sweet 'stache

50 Badass Mustaches and the Faces Who Sport Them

Jon Chattman and Rich Tarantino
Foreword by John Oates
ILLUSTRATED BY BRETT UNDERHILL

Published by
Adams Media, a division of F+W Media, Inc.
57 Littlefield Street, Avon, MA 02322. U.S.A.
www.adamsmedia.com

ISBN 10: 1-4405-0144-0
ISBN 13: 978-1-4405-0144-9

Printed in the United States of America.

J I H G F E D C B A

Library of Congress Cataloging-in-Publication Data
is available from the publisher.

This publication is designed to provide accurate and authoritative information with
regard to the subject matter covered. It is sold with the understanding that the publisher is not engaged in rendering legal, accounting, or other professional advice. If
legal advice or other expert assistance is required, the services of a competent professional person should be sought.
   —From a *Declaration of Principles* jointly adopted by a Committee of the
American Bar Association and a Committee of Publishers and Associations

Many of the designations used by manufacturers and sellers to distinguish their prod-
uct are claimed as trademarks. Where those designations appear in this book and
Adams Media was aware of a trademark claim, the designations have been printed with
initial capital letters.

This book is available at quantity discounts for bulk purchases.

For information, please call 1-800-289-0963.

What They're Saying about *Sweet 'Stache*

"If you read only ONE book about pop culture mustaches let it be this one. . . . Unless you can find another one but I highly doubt it. Chattman and Tarantino are the Woodward and the Bernstein of pop culture mustaches."

—Paul Scheer, MTV's *Human Giant*

"A mustache book has redeeming social values as a cautionary tale: proving not everybody looks good with one!"

—Alan Thicke, *Growing Pains*

"The facial hair book of the year! This is without a doubt the finest book on facial hair I have ever read. I await the authors' tome on 'nose hairs' with eager anticipation."

—Brian Kiley, Emmy Award–winning writer of
Late Night with Conan O'Brien

"A funny thing happened to me on my way into the jungle one day. I spied a monkey with a long, flowing handlebar mustache! It was an emperor tamarin, and I really have no idea why this diminutive monkey was sporting such a push broom. I guess I'll have to pick up *'Sweet Stache* to understand why!"

—Jack Hanna, Director Emeritus, Columbus Zoo,
and television wild-animal correspondent

"Soup-straining reads like *'Sweet Stache*, are helping the mustache experience a modern-day renaissance after cookie dusters nearly disappeared from existence at the tail end of the 1970s."

—Aaron Perlut, executive director of the American Mustache Institute

"The journey of growing and cultivating a mustache is one you can live your whole life. It only gets better with every mustache. In 'Sweet Stache we learn of the legacy of the mustache, and the men who have helped pave the road for a brighter, hairier, and more lip-conscious future. . . . First it grows on you—then it grows on everyone else. I'm talking about the mustache . . . and also this amazing collection of mustaches—known as 'Sweet Stache."

—Jay Della Valle, director/producer of the documentary,
The Glorius Mustache Challenge

"I thought I knew everything about mustaches . . . I mean, I am gay with cable . . . then I read 'Sweet Stache."

—ANT, host of *Last Comic Standing* and VH-1's *Celebrity Fit Club*

"Reflecting back through the greats of 'stache history, many names come to mind—Frank Viola, Keith Hernandez, Don Mattingly, our dads, and even the Hulkster himself Hulk Hogan. While each man rocks a different facial hair sculpture, one fact remains constant among them. . . . A man with a good 'stache, is a good-stached man . . . and a good-stached man with this book is even cooler."

—Covino, Rich, and Spot of *The Covino & Rich Show*
on Sirius XM Satellite Radio

"If you read only one book on celebrity facial hair this year, make it this one. I promise you will never look at mustaches or celebrities or books the same way ever again."

—Richard Dresser, playwright and television writer
(*Good Vibrations*, *Below the Belt*, and *The Days and Nights of Molly Dodd*)

"There are celebrity mug shots everywhere. You see hair and makeup publications and TV shows all the time. Sure, how about focusing on that caterpillar? It's right there in the center—bull's eye—twelve o' clock right in the middle of their face. I'm going to have to go with Tom Selleck having the best mustache ever, because it totally dominated anything else that he ever did. That's all I will ever remember him for is that mustache first, and his Hawaiian shirt second."

—Rob Van Dam, innovative wrestler
and host of RVD TV on robvandam.com

"[This book] is here to help. Facial hair can be traumatic when left undefined. Hector Aranguren, my Colombian best friend, had a black mustache and a deep voice by eleven years old. It would be six years before I sprouted two small pale whiskers on my own lip, and he teased me for that entire time. He is currently in jail for selling cocaine."

—Greg Fitzsimmons, comedian and Emmy Award–winning writer

"I hate facial hair (unless it's on Johnny Depp), but I love this book."

—Comedienne Wendy Liebman

"*Sweet 'Stache* is—without question—the best mustache book the world has ever seen. For years I have worn a goatee, but thanks to Chattman and Tarantino's hairy findings, I plan on immediately rushing to the nearest barber and asking for a 'John Oates.'"

—Jeff Pearlman, *New York Times* best-selling author of
Boys Will Be Boys and *The Bad Guys Won*

"As we all know, education saves lives, and this book is no different. It is only in our very recent history in the age of the modern man where the mustache has not had such a comfortable place in certain parts of the world. Just as my charity work for Movember unites the world again with the mustache to fight for greater men's health through a month-long growing journey, this book will do the same. It is *The Great Gatsby* of mustaches, and soon enough there will be fountains of hair spilling from the upper lips of men everywhere as the inspiring words in these pages spread to finally help people understand where the mustache belongs... worn proud among the beautiful men of this world. The heart of man's health is his 'mo.' Just like a Labrador, a luxurious mustache shows the good health and great lover that he is. May your sausages be hot and your 'mo' thick."

—Jim BBQ, Movember international grooming ambassador
(Movember.com)

"This book fills a much-needed void. It's a necessary one in the annals of literature. My own personal favorite celebrity mustache would be Groucho Marx's. To watch this middle-aged man smoking his cigar, batting his eyebrows, and chasing young women around sans the mustache just would not feel right. Groucho Marx gave me many hours of pleasure with his movies, and *'Sweet Stache*, I am sure, will bring you lots of pleasure, too."

—Eddie Deezen, actor in *Grease 2*,
Midnight Madness, and voice-over talent

Dedication

Jon Chattman and Rich Tarantino wish to dedicate this book to their families, their spouses, and all of those who helped get this out there. The authors would like to dedicate this book to their fathers, in particular, for being such great role models, and at one point in their lives, sporting the sweetest 'staches of all.

Contents

A Foreword by John Oates **xi**

An Introduction by Jon Chattman **xv**

Mustache Growth over the Years **xviii**

The 'Stache-o-Meter **xxii**

The Sweet 'Staches

Epilogue

A Foreword by John Oates

I couldn't wait to grow a mustache. I stopped shaving my upper lip the day I graduated from high school. By the time I was ready to enter college the following September, I had a sparse, vestigial growth of dark hair sprouting due south of my nose. Though I cannot recall the exact date, I can never forget the deep-seated motivation for this tonsorial compulsion. On the surface, I am sure it was somewhat inspired by the desire to look older and more mature . . . but if I had to delve, it was probably more driven by the fact that I always hated my upper lip and the way I looked when I smiled.

In fact, having a mustache and never smiling became a permanent component of my persona through the quaintly self-important decade of the seventies. Enter the big eighties and, symbolic of the zeitgeist of the era, my facial hair grew denser and more imposing, and like the supernova that was my career, the 'stache seemed to explode from my face, luminous and larger than life itself . . . but still no smile.

Now in retrospect, I can see that my personality and my mustache had become intrinsically linked. That dark swath of hair became my living logo. As I begat the 'stache, the mustache became me, symbolically thrusting forward from its prominence in the center of my countenance. A flying buttress of follicles projecting my power and personality out to the world that fell before it. More than a hairstyle or a beard, the mighty mustache became somehow much more than a mere personal grooming choice . . . moreover, it conveyed a subtly threatening and unyielding masculine image, complex in its message and undeniable in its statement.

So for over two decades I bore that albatross noir through the protracted adolescence known as pop stardom. From every angle, in every photograph, bopping through every silly '80s MTV moment, my mustache became my marquee, until I could not distinguish between it and me. Then I changed. . . .

In 1990, there occurred a life-altering convergence of circumstances, dusted with a sprinkling of fate, which led to a quantum collapse of many close relationships, both business and personal. The resulting mid-life revelation finally shook me from my childlike stupor, and one night, bathed in the light of where my future might lead me . . . I stared at a mustache on a stranger's face reflected in the mirror of a Tokyo Hotel room. Then, at that moment, with total commitment and trembling hand, I knew what I must do . . .

the 'stache had to go. The act itself, the stroke of the blade, was surprisingly simple, but as the shaving continued, the cutting began to take on a ritualistic gravitas . . . for as the hair fell away, from the chrysalis emerged a man.

No longer possessed by the power of the 'stache, I was reborn, wriggled out from under the skin of that mustachioed character, and for the first time in so many years . . .

I began to smile.

—John Oates, music and mustache legend

An Introduction by Jon Chattman

I worked as a counselor at a Westchester County, New York, day camp for nearly a decade. While there, I had my handful of kids to look after, but I also fulfilled my love for writing by running the camp newspaper. I made many friends, but struck out with a lot of women. (Let's not focus on the latter.) One person I befriended between swims at the pool and arts-and-crafts projects is the coauthor of this book, Rich Tarantino.

In the summer of 1995, I enlisted Rich, a fellow counselor who worked with younger kids, as a contributor to the camp newspaper. I dubbed his column "Cheek to Cheek," which was a quirky Q&A

and a sendup of yet another counselor column named "Eye to Eye," which was inspired by, but had absolutely nothing to do with, Connie Chung.

"Cheek to Cheek" didn't explore anything newsworthy either. It was as inane as you could get. The questions and answers usually revolved around wrestling and toasted ravioli appetizers at a local diner. As a gag, a photo of Rich didn't accompany the article. Instead, a really crappy clip-art drawing of the infamous Burt Reynolds was featured. Why? It just seemed right. The column was goofy. Rich was goofy. I was goofy. It just worked. That clip-art and the column ran year after year for five years. Then, like Burt Reynolds's career, it faded when we both bolted from the camp.

"Burt," however, made quite a comeback in the 2000s. The name, later changed to *bert* for obvious reasons you'll find out shortly, became a term Rich and I used to refer to men's mustaches. It all started for a handful of reasons, most notably "Cheek to Cheek's" Burt Reynolds had a "bert" and Rich's friend, Bert, had a "bert." The term has been a part of our vocabulary since, and our friends have helped exploit it as well. It's quite common to hear, "Check out that guy's bert!" after a man with a mustache walks by any of us. Purchasing self-adhesive mustaches has also become a trend for us. Were we popular? No. But we all amused each other, and that was most important.

By October 2005, we took the bert bonanza global. I enlisted Rich to help me create a website entitled TheCheapPop.com to profile mustaches and feature humor and pop culture icons as well. We created the "'Stache-o-Meter," a rating system for famous people with mustaches. Stars were judged on the quality and durability of their mustache's longevity and overall facial appeal. John Oates, for example, could've been a solid 10, but because he shaved his mustache during the course of his career, he instantly lost mustache street cred. The website also included a television and film database ("databert") of actors who grew mustaches or put fake ones on for respective parts. Johnny Depp had a bert in *Donnie Brasco*, but did you know Ethan Hawke had one in the little-seen flick *The Newton Boys*? Didn't think so. That brings us back to the book's concept. Why the interest in men's mustaches? Mustaches have been an integral part of Americana, and once you read this book, you will realize their importance and never quite look at facial hair the same way again.

Mustache Growth over the Years

mus·tache also mous·tache: the hair that grows on the human upper lip, especially when groomed.

Throughout history, men have been upstaged by their mustaches. Sure, Sir Thomas More was beheaded after refusing to join Henry VIII's Church of England, but first, he refused to shave. Similarly, Fred the Baker, of Dunkin Donuts' TV commercial fame, always looked exhausted after waking up so early to "make the donuts," but while the bags under his eyes suggested 5 A.M., his mustache always looked high-noon. And what about Lionel Richie? He toured with the Commodores, made "Endless Love" with Diana Ross, and helped unite nations in 1985 with "We Are the World." But he'll always be recognized as that singer who went "Dancing on the Ceiling" with a finger-length mustache on his face.

While mustaches, or *berts* (a bastardization of "Burt," as previously mentioned), have been around long before Wilford Brimley started whoring out oatmeal, oftentimes they have been the underdog of a man's face—having to fight to get noticed and appreciated. This book champions their cause. It showcases fifty men—from the world of entertainment, history, and sports—who have their own unique 'stache style, documenting the good, the bad, and the hairy. That's what is amazing about mustaches. They come in all shapes and sizes, and they often define the man (and in some cases, the lady), his face, and his stardom.

They can be a perfect triangle, like 1980s newsman Roland Smith's (perhaps an inspiration for *Anchorman*'s Ron Burgundy), or come with a curly finish like pitcher Rollie Fingers's spaghetti-style 'stache. A mustache can be as thick as a walrus's, like philosopher Friedrich Nietzsche's, or as pencil-thin as the line above director John Waters's lip. Stars like these didn't bow down to the pressures of societal or social trends. Whether it was displayed on film or television, on the Broadway stage, on the sports field, or better yet, while enjoying off-camera moments in their everyday lives, these gents accentuated their philtrums with some glorious fuzz. Maybe they just plain liked the look, or perhaps the touch that only a mustache could give them.

It can be said that behind every great man, there's a great mustache. Well, not exactly. But if we had our way, that statement would be emblazoned in every history book. A mustache builds character, adds life to an otherwise empty face, and can signify a key moment in history simply by its size and scope.

When Theodore "Teddy" Roosevelt charged up San Juan Hill on July 1, 1898, he led by example—not with his fighting spirit, but with a menacing, bushy mustache. The Rough Rider's bristles were fittingly rough around the edges and stood firm, just like the man himself. Facial hair instantly gave credibility to a man who wouldn't seem as intimidating without it.

Similarly, Adolf Hitler stole Charlie Chaplin's toothbrush-style mustache and made it somewhat a symbol of his power (and insanity). One wonders how seriously the dictator would've been taken if he had Charles Barkley's weak mustache instead of the stately fur popularized by the silent film star. On a related note, Robert Baden-Powell began the Boy Scouts movement in 1908, but one wonders if he could've found the funding without the appeal of his well-disciplined 'stache.

Oftentimes, a mustache isn't grown for a keen fashion sense; it's grown to make a statement. John Lennon led the Beatles in shedding their wholesome looks by growing unrecognizably thick mustaches (and ultimately, beards). Similarly, Albert Einstein and Salvador Dali each had uncharacteristic mustaches on their faces to add credibility to their genius. It was as if they were saying to the general public, "Hey, we've got crazy-looking mustaches; but it doesn't matter because we're geniuses!" Another great man in history, Christopher Hewitt, made his finely groomed mustache do the talking as Mr. Belvedere. His 'stache set the tone right away. Like the British housekeeper himself, his mustache was neat, nicely put together, and not to be messed with by pesky American kids.

A mustache can also be a sign of the times. When looked at in retrospect, it can automatically transport you back to a historical moment. For example, when we watch a Cheech and Chong movie, *Sonny and Cher Show* reruns, or a pornography classic starring the immortal Harry Reems, we're instantly taken back to the 1970s. Together with the late 1960s, this was a time of free love, long sideburns, and thick, straggly mustaches. By comparison, when we see a picture of a man with a thick Fu Manchu, we know it belongs to the era of Genghis Khan's Mongolian Empire or the latter days of Pancho Villa's nineteenth century. This is because no one in their right mind would leave the house looking like that today. However, there was a time when baseball slugger Mike Piazza came close to revitalizing its hoary legacy. But he never grew his out that far.

Speaking of baseball's grooming elite, frequently players will grow unique variations of a mustache simply to stand out and get noticed—or to intimidate. In fact, growing a bizarre mustache must be in the MLB rule book, under the section for relief pitching. Don Aase wasn't a sensational pitcher, but deserved back-page headlines more for that big old bushy mustache than any fastball he threw.

Examples of the importance of mustaches could go on forever. There are few precious things in life that are timeless. And as the above men point out clearly, mustaches are one of them.

Author Rudyard Kipling once said, "Being kissed by a man who didn't wax his mustache was like eating an egg without salt."

We have no clue what that means, but we're sure it's sound advice. To us, men with mustaches often have more personality above their lip than in their entire body.

This is their story. . . .

The 'Stache-o-Meter

What you are about to read is highly classified. The 'Stache-o-Meter marks the end of a decade's worth of preparation by self-professed mustacheologists Jon Chattman and Rich Tarantino, who carefully researched facial hair growth and techniques throughout the 1990s in a hidden laboratory in Geneva. What you are about to read is highly classified.

With the goal of creating the world's first and only mustache scoring system, the two dedicated a good six and a half years of their lives to examining specimens, particles, and mustache matter. Using high-tech equipment that we're not permitted to describe here, the two discovered a way in which individual men can maximize their mustache growth. Keeping that in mind, and taking Neolithic times into account, the two created the 'Stache-o-Meter, which rates men on their individual mustache achievement based on their MGP (Mustache Growth Potential). While we can't tell you about the MGP directly, we can say it takes into consideration all factors of an individual's genetic makeup in deciding their ultimate rank on the 'Stache-o-Meter.

To put it simply, the 'Stache-o-Meter is a ten-point rating scale that takes into account the following five elements in its composite score:

Attitude: What can be better than sporting a badass 'stache? For years, the mustache has been a symbol of power, dominance, and a never-say-die existence.

Most notable: Dick Butkus, the Iron Sheik, and *Police Academy* alum Bubba Smith

Longevity: Fads come and go but nothing is more timeless than a thick, fuzzy mustache. This particular criterion is based on the amount of years and work put into the many facets of some very fine facial hair. (Say *that* five times fast!)

Most notable: Tom Selleck, Muhammad Iqbal, and basketball founder Dr. James Naismith

Style: Pimpin' ain't easy, but neither is growing the perfect push broom. When it comes to setting the standard and reaching new heights, it's simple: It's not the man that makes the mustache, it's the mustache that makes the man.

Most notable: Richard Roundtree, *Star Trek*'s James "Scotty" Doohan, and the guy on the Pringles carton

Creativity: Many artists, actors, writers, and designers go into their respective fields because it's a source of constant creative expression. Similarly, many grow facial hair to express themselves and add to their already unique persona.

Most notable: Salvador Dali, Pancho Villa, and timelessly annoying comedian Rip Taylor

Overall Appeal: From dictators to U.S. presidents to kung-fu stars, it's clear that great men require great mustaches. Gabe Kaplan of *Welcome Back, Kotter* may be considered to have a great mustache, but his track record after the show isn't a ringing endorsement for the man himself.

Most notable: Josef Stalin, William H. Taft, and *Delta Force*'s Chuck Norris

Because of the magnitude and demand for facial hair, the mustache will always be the bridge between boyhood and grown man. Similarly, the 'Stache-o-Meter is the bridge between a somewhat mediocre mustache and a definitive revolutionary mustache. Naturally, it's graded on a curve.

the sweet 'staches

Larry Bird

Technical Fowl

Larry Bird's unflappable fuzz and unstoppable three-point shooting precision have made him one of the most recognized athletes in the past thirty years. The blond-haired shooting whiz from French Lick, Indiana, helped put the National Basketball Association back on the map during the glory days of the 1980s.

Of course, "Larry Legend" was not alone among hardwood heroes in short shorts. Among the many mustachioed contemporaries to share the rock with "The Hick from French Lick" during the NBA's revitalizing resurgence into mainstream sports during this period were elite hoopsters Hakeem Olajuwon, "Dr. J." Julius Erving, and the unstoppable Kelly Tripuka.

Before entering the NBA, Bird honed his basketball skills at Indiana State University, where he led the team to a National Championship game, only to come up short against Earvin Johnson and Michigan State. "Magic" would later join the Los Angeles Lakers, which had its very own "showtime" fast-break style of ball playing that was also led by a 'stache-sporting supporting cast of Kareem Abdul-Jabbar, A. C. Green, and Michael Cooper, just to name a few.

Bird's bert in all its blond glory helped lead the gritty and tough Boston Celtics to the NBA finals, making Lakers versus Celtics one of the sports world's top marquee matchups. Bird's performances in the clutch in that series and over a thirteen-year career helped lead Celtic Pride to three world championships in the *Max Headroom* decade. Along the way, Bird was selected to twelve all-star games, landed three MVP trophies, and even took on a mustache-wearing Michael Jordan in a Grimace-less Big Mac challenge on the hardwood. A consummate team player and deadly shooter, Bird's efforts are forever immortalized in Springfield, Massachusetts, at the Basketball Hall of Fame, along with basketball inventor Dr. James Naismith and Wilt Chamberlain, a man who just so happened to be rocking a very prominent patch of hair above his lip the night he poured down 100 points against the Warriors.

Bird capped off his illustrious year with an Olympic Gold medal with the "Dream Team" in 1992, and ever since then, has been spreading his wings as an NBA coach and top executive in the game. The only problem with that last sentence is that he, for the most part, left his bert in Boston. For nearly two decades, Bird has tossed up a brick and flown the facial hair coop. We choose to remember the good old days when Bird's bert resembled Mr. McFeeley's mustache from *Mr. Rogers' Neighborhood* combined with the texture and toughness of Governor Jesse "The Body" Ventura's governing grizzle.

'Stache-o-Meter Rating

Larry Bird and his buzzer-beating bert were a winning combination, but as his retired jersey hangs in the Boston rafters, his retired Hall-of-Fame mustache no longer hangs from his legendary nose. That mustache was fourth-quarter clutch all the way. Because he decided to retire the Spalding in favor of the Bic, he nets just a 6.5 on the 'Stache-o-Meter. Instead of being nothing but net, he's become nothing but bald under his nose.

TOP FIVE NBA
WEST COAST WHISKERS

1. BRAD DAVIS

2. KAREEM ABDUL-JABBAR

3. SARUNAS MARCIULIONIS

4. KURT RAMBIS

5. ROLANDO BLACKMAN

Wilford Brimley

Handle(bar) with Care

Don Ameche may have danced his way to an Oscar in 1985's *Cocoon*, but Wilford Brimley danced his way into our hearts in that same Ron Howard–directed elderly love fest. How'd he do it? He bluntly talked about flatulence. As Ben Luckett, a skeptical, cantankerous older man, he noted to his character's grandson that he couldn't eat Italian food because it gave him gas. Iconic quips aside, there's more to this legendary character actor than nailing punch lines and playing crabby old farts. Perhaps not, but we digress.

For decades, Brimley has enriched quality films like *The China Syndrome* and *Absence of Malice* with his signature curmudgeon style, but all the while, he's done so with a jaw-dropping hairy handlebar mustache that is just as gruff as the man himself.

The Salt Lake City–born native has been a fixture in pop culture for the better part of five decades, but it wasn't always that way. A former Marine, Brimley originally worked as a rodeo rider and blacksmith before becoming a bodyguard for eccentric millionaire (and fellow mustache supporter) Howard Hughes. The acting bug didn't bite Brimley until the 1960s when he appeared as an extra and a stunt man in television westerns. While he dabbled with acting, he didn't really hit his stride until the 1980s when he appeared in hit after hit, including the aforementioned *Cocoon*, *The Natural* (who could ever forget the fair-hair double-play tandem of Brimley and Richard Farnsworth?), and the action-comedy *Remo Williams*.

Brimley also charmed audiences on the small screen playing a guardian to kids, including a pre-*Playboy* and unstable Shannen Doherty on *Our House*, and some crusty old guy of Endor in George Lucas's TV-movie *Ewoks: The Battle of Endor*. In the 1990s, he turned in two fine performances as a U.S. postmaster general in an episode of *Seinfeld* and as a chilling security expert in the Tom Cruise action drama *The Firm*.

But let's face it—Brimley's greatest claim to fame has been as the spokesman for Quaker Oats in the 1980s and 1990s and for the gratuitous fuzz that's protruded from under his nose for as long as we've known him. Mustached Brimley is Jim Henson's Statler (of Statler and Waldorf fame) come to life and just as cranky. Thick and grainy like Grizzly Adams (and similar in color depending on the film—sometimes white, other times gray with strands of mustard yellow), the Brimley bert looks as if someone crammed Sam Elliott's mustache and a Furby together right under the man's nose. Having said all that, it's pretty clear that when it comes to mustaches and oatmeal, Brimley knows "the right thing to do and the tasty way to do it."

'Stache-o-Meter Rating

Whether it's advocating diabetes testing supplies for Liberty Medical or more controversial subjects like horse-race gambling, cockfighting, and Senator John McCain in his 2008 bid for the White House, Wilford Brimley has never shied away from lending his support to causes he believes in. Fittingly, his walrus mustache has gone to great lengths to support his face. Brimley scores a 9 on the 'Stache-o-Meter for the size and scope of his 'stache. If the man ran for public office strictly on a mustache platform, it'd be a no-brainer who'd win the ticket. His mustache is a gas.

TOP FIVE
GRUMPY OLD 'STACHES

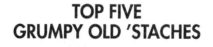

1. WILFORD BRIMLEY

2. *MONOPOLY'S* RICH UNCLE PENNYBAGS

3. LEN LESSER, *SEINFELD'S* "UNCLE LEO"

4. SEAN CONNERY

5. OSSIE DAVIS

Keep Your Eyes on the Ball, Bill. . . . We'll Focus on the 'Stache

He played for the Chicago Cubs and the Boston Red Sox—two baseball franchises most often associated with being cursed. But Bill Buckner was a truly blessed man. Blessed with a scruffy mustache, that is.

"Billy Buck" seemed to have it all when he came up to the majors with the Los Angeles Dodgers during the 1969 season. Coincidentally, it was the same year the New York Mets took home their first World Series Championship. Buckner could hit, run, and field well. But as highlight reels have shown over the last twenty years, Buckner's career went down the toilet when he let Mookie Wilson's duck-fart groundball slip between his legs during the 1986 World Series.

Forever known as a goat, we recognize Buckner not just for his unappreciated efforts on the field (he had 2,500-plus hits), but for the figurative balls he had to share a Fenway locker room with fellow mustache owners Jim Rice, Wade Boggs, and Dwight Evans. His mustache shared traits with all of his fellow Beantown bert brethren, but it came off far more rough around the edges—literally. Buckner wasn't a slugger, but to us, he'll forever be the Sultan of 'Stache.

'Stache-o-Meter Rating

Bill Buckner famously took his eyes off the ball, but ours were glued to his mustache. For his efforts on the field and above his mouth, he scores a solid 8.5 on the 'Stache-o-Meter. He may have cursed the Cubbies and the Sox, but curses to Bill if he ever shaves his sweet-swinging stubble!

TOP TEN MUSTACHED
FIRST BASEMEN

1. KEITH HERNANDEZ
2. SID BREAM
3. BILL BUCKNER
4. DON MATTINGLY
5. DAN BROUTHERS
6. WILLIE STARGELL
7. RAFAEL PALMEIRO
8. EDDIE MURRAY
9. STEVE BALBONI
10. GLENN DAVIS

TOP TEN MLB PITCHERS WITH MUSTACHES

1. WILLIE HERNANDEZ
2. "GOOSE" GOSSAGE
3. ROLLIE FINGERS
4. PETE VUKOVICH
5. JERRY REUSS
6. LAMAR HOYT
7. DENNIS ECKERSLEY
8. ROD BECK
9. DON AASE
10. DAVE STIEB

A Silent but Deadly 'Stache

Charlie Chaplin was one of the most prolific talents the world has ever seen. A versatile performer, he wrote, produced, directed, and even scored the music for his motion pictures in a career that spanned over sixty-five years. Best known for his alter ego, "The Little Tramp," he became a legend by expressing himself without words and strutting around with a cane, a slim-fitted coat, baggy trousers, and a signature toothbrush mustache. Let's just say the latter spoke volumes for the silent film star.

Mimicked by a fascist pig and an overweight sidekick—Adolf Hitler and Oliver Hardy respectively—Chaplin's mustache was a piece of fluffy goodness that could never be duplicated. It looked like a black cotton ball smack dab under his nose, and up until that infamous dictator grew one of his own, it was as delightful as child star Jackie Coogan.

Chaplin's importance and influence extends far beyond facial fury. Born in London, the performer fought his way out of a troubled childhood in an impoverished London neighborhood, and quickly made a name for himself on the vaudeville stage and in motion pictures. Some masterful works include *The Kid*, *The Gold Rush*, *City Lights*, and the socially conscious *Modern Times* and *The Great Dictator*; the latter being a satire on Hitler.

While success always found Chaplin on screen, off camera was a different story. He often found himself in bad relationships (he was married four times), and he went through a series of scandals, including a paternity suit in 1943.

He eventually fled to Switzerland amid immigration issues, tax problems, and other trials and tribulations, but he continued to work—writing books and memoirs, and returning to Los Angeles in 1972 to accept a special lifetime Oscar. He died in 1977, mercifully never having had to sit through Richard Attenborough's painfully boring bio-flick about his life.

'Stache-o-Meter Rating

For its originality and pre-Hitler existence, we give Chaplin's facial patch an 8 on the 'Stache-o-Meter. It's rumored Adolf Hitler modeled his mustache after Chaplin, because he wanted similar worldwide attention and acclaim. He didn't succeed, and his actions only served to end what could've been a perfectly good mustache style for everyone else.

TOP FIVE DICTATORS WITH MUSTACHES

1. ADOLF HITLER

2. SADDAM HUSSEIN

3. JOSEF STALIN

4. PRESIDENT SKROOB

5. RAUL CASTRO

TOP FIVE RANDOM BRITS WITH BERTS

1. FREDDIE MERCURY

2. JOHN CLEESE

3. TERRY-THOMAS

4. DAVID NIVEN

5. SACHA BARON COHEN

Baddest Mustache in the Whole Damn Town

Jim Croce's mustache was the antithesis of the man and his music. While the singer/songwriter's tunes were always as honest and upbeat as he was, the Croce 'stache was a grizzly bear: an uncompromising and often distressing fleece coat that never seemed properly groomed and always came off angrier than Leroy Brown.

While that no-nonsense mustache resonates even by today's standards, Croce made more of an impact with his music in the 1970s. The performer grew up a musical child in South Philadelphia, learning to play the accordion at five years old. While he always had a love for melody, Croce didn't truly go into the music business until college. While attending Villanova College in Pennsylvania, he formed various bands and was a fixture playing frat parties. After meeting his wife, Ingrid, he started playing gigs and worked the coffeehouse circuit with her as a duo. The two eventually moved to New York to record an album, but when the money got tight, they returned to the Keystone State for a more suburban life.

To make ends meet, Croce worked construction and did some bit vocal work for commercials, but he never lost sight of his first love. Eventually, his perseverance paid off, and he landed a three-record deal with ABC—the company, not the crappy 1980s band of the same name. *You Don't Mess Around with Jim* and *Life and Times* were his first two albums, which both took off instantly.

Croce scored such hits as "You Don't Mess Around with Jim," "Operator (That's Not the Way It Feels)," and "Time in a Bottle," but his biggest single was "Bad, Bad Leroy Brown." It hit number one on the charts, selling 2 million copies, and possibly inspired classic wrestler Junkyard Dog to choose his in-ring moniker. (On an unrelated note, we have no idea what that grappler's song "Grab Them Cakes" meant.)

Tragically, on September 20, 1973, Croce, just thirty, and collaborator Maury Muehleisen, only twenty-four, perished in a plane crash—only one day before Croce's third album, *I Got a Name*, was to be released. Following his death, the musician scored more hit singles including the title track, "Workin' at the Car Wash Blues," and "I'll Have to Say I Love You in a Song." The poignant "Bottle" was subsequently rereleased and hit number one as well.

One can only imagine how many more hit records Croce would've put out had he not died in the prime of his career. To a lesser degree, one can't help but imagine how his mustache would've evolved. As it stood, the Croce 'stache evolved throughout his years of fame.

Sometimes his 'stache was a thick triangle in the mold of Oscar the Grouch's eyebrows, while other times it was equipped with a soul patch, à la Frank Zappa. On some occasions, it even extended to an uncompleted handlebar, à la Rob Schneider's *50 First Dates* facial experiment. No matter how he wore it, the mustache, like the man, never let us down.

'Stache-o-Meter Rating

While he's been gone for over three decades, Jim Croce's music continues to inspire us today. So does that bad, bad 'stache. For its unflinching whiskers and width, the Croce mustache ranks a solid 8.5 on the 'Stache-o-Meter. If we could save time in a bottle, the first thing we'd do is save every day Croce wore a mustache on his face, and his heart on his sleeve.

TOP FIVE MODERN ROCKIN' 'STACHES NOT AS BADASS AS CROCE'S

1. NICK CAVE

2. GASPARD AUGÉ, JUSTICE

3. RIVERS CUOMO, WEEZER

4. CHRIS CAIN, WE ARE SCIENTISTS

5. CHRIS ROSS, WOLFMOTHER

David Crosby

That's One Far-Out Mustache

He was one-third of arguably the most famous trio in rock and roll history. He's an honored singer and songwriter, an occasional bad actor, a sperm donor to lesbians, and probably smokes more weed than Snoop Dogg on a Saturday night and drinks more than Mickey Mantle did between a Tuesday doubleheader. But, for all of David Crosby's career accomplishments, nothing stands out more than that big hunk of chunk over his mouth.

A cross between Dick Van Dyke's *Diagnosis Murder* 'stache and Macy Gray's afro, the Crosby, Stills, and Nash harmonizer's bushy mustache is music to everyone's eyes. It hangs as loose and free as those hippie chicks at Woodstock. As a matter of fact, industry

17

insiders say Crosby's mustache of 1969 actually measured larger in diameter than his beer gut of 1978.

Let's face it though—Crosby's more than just a mustache. After dropping out of drama class, he quickly established himself as a force in the music industry by helping form the Byrds, a group best known for their cover of Bob Dylan's "Mr. Tambourine Man" (and to a lesser degree, for spelling *bird* with a *y*). After he was booted from the Byrds, our hairy hero met Buffalo Springfield's Stephen Stills at a party hosted by Mama Cass, and the two soon joined forces with equally established rocker Graham Nash. Their self-titled disc was an instant hit, and "by the time they got to Woodstock," joined by Neil Young, they were already legends.

Throughout the years (with or without CSN or CSNY), Crosby has been responsible for countless classic hit songs, including "Our House," "Teach Your Children," and "Déjà Vu." The group was fittingly inducted into the Rock and Roll Hall of Fame in 1997. It's also fitting that a once-mustachioed James Taylor inducted them. After all, Crosby paved the way for performers like him, and from what we remember, that folk singer saw fire, rain, and facial hair back in the day.

As the years have gone by, success has found Crosby off stage, out of the studio, and away from his band mates. He's dabbled in acting, appearing in such shows as *Roseanne* and films like *Backdraft*; has made headlines for his health woes (who could forget that famous liver transplant); and made headlines when he pleasured himself in a Dixie cup. His sperm was responsible for knocking up Melissa Etheridge's then-partner Julie Cypher not once, but two times. If only Crosby donated parts of his mustache to impotent mustache growers like Donald Faison of *Scrubs* and Jose Canseco's 1986 Donruss rookie card.

'Stache-o-Meter Rating

Woodstock will arguably be remembered most for Jimi Hendrix's "Star-Spangled Banner," but this book isn't about tripped-out guitar riffs. So Crosby's authentic and far-out mustache earns him a solid 9 on the 'Stache-o-Meter. We'll deduct a point for his decision to join a band called David and the Dorks and for not renaming the band Crosby, Stills, and 'Stache. David Crosby once recorded a popular song called "Almost Cut My Hair." Thankfully, he never trimmed his bush.

TOP TEN FAT GUYS WITH PHAT MUSTACHES

1. DAVID CROSBY

2. FATS DOMINO

3. RON JEREMY

4. MARLON BRANDO

5. WILFORD BRIMLEY

6. CHRIS "DA BEARS" FARLEY

7. PHILADELPHIA EAGLES COACH ANDY REID

8. *CHIP AND DALE'S RESCUE RANGERS'* FAT CAT

9. PITCHER DAVID WELLS

10. WILLIAM CONRAD

Salvador Dalí

Facial Strokes of Genius

Whether it's putting together a portfolio of work including paint-ings, sculptures, photography, and films, or being known simply as a true eccentric (and we don't mean that in a Michael Jackson sort of way), Salvador Dalí is considered one of the most influential artists of the twentieth century. The Spanish-born trendsetter, who produced over 1,500 paintings in his lifetime, is arguably best known for his symbolic and surrealistic *The Persistence of Memory*, which was completed in 1931. Sure he was a genius with an uncanny talent, but we'd consider Dalí's signature 'stache to be the true work of art.

It's said his flamboyant fuzz was grown in tribute to fellow Spaniard Diego Velazquez, who painted the court of Philip IV back in the day (those royal whiskers are also worth mentioning). Paying great attention to detail, much like all of his masterpieces, Dalí's mustache contained brushstrokes of genius, highlighted by long curly points at each end. Combining the spaghetti elements of Gogol Bordello front man Eugene Hutz with the pencil-thin Vaseline-texture of a Chuck Berry, the Salvador 'stache can take Van Gogh's missing ear any day in the battle of best artistic accessories.

Dalí's facial hair couldn't have looked any better even if he painted it on himself, and that's why we'd go so far as to say it's the most important push broom in the last century. (Our sincere apologies to the late and highly talented Luther Vandross.)

'Stache-o-Meter Rating

There's no mistaking the genius of Salvador Dalí's body of work, but we cannot forget that man's magnificent mustache. For its style, originality, and elevation, this surrealist 'stache earns a respectable 8.5 on the 'Stache-o-Meter. Dalí's mustache was like seeing Snidely Whiplash's villainous mustache from *Dudley Do-Right* brought to life. Only, Dalí's was more animated.

TOP TEN CREATIVE GENIUSES WITH CREATIVE MUSTACHES

1. SALVADOR DALÍ

2. ALBERT EINSTEIN

3. ORVILLE WRIGHT

4. THOMAS HARDY

5. EDGAR ALLAN POE

6. MARK TWAIN

7. FRIEDRICH NIETZSCHE

8. JOHN LENNON

9. JOHN WATERS

10. STAN LEE

A Candy Man with a Sweet 'Stache

In a career that spanned roughly six decades, Sammy Davis Jr. entertained audiences with his infectious personality, trademark singing voice, and classic comedic timing.

The groundbreaking performer was admired for the famous friends he performed with and the company he kept (seriously, would you willingly hang out with Jerry Lewis?), overcoming a car accident that claimed his left eye, and speaking out against the injustices to his race. To us, he'll always be remembered for breaking out of the Rat Pack and coming into his own with some furry face candy.

Davis's mustache was always the star attraction, whether he performed in Vegas or abroad, and it upstaged those odd turtlenecks he used to wear as well as the assorted bling that hung around his neck or on his fingers, and even the glass eye implanted in his socket.

Born in Harlem in 1925, Davis spent most of his early years learning dance and entertaining from his father. After serving in the army during World War II, where he performed for his fellow soldiers, he landed on Broadway. By 1959, he had become a member of the "Rat Pack," along with legendary performers Dean Martin, Frank Sinatra, Joey Bishop, and some British guy named Peter Lawford. He further crossed the color barrier by headlining shows in Vegas hotels, and becoming a star in his own right.

The performer dabbled with film and television work in the 1960s, and scored a few radio-friendly songs like "I've Gotta Be Me," "Candy Man," and the theme song from a pre–*Money Train* and trial-bound Robert Blake *Baretta*. Like that latter song said, Davis had the "eye of the sparrow" (whatever that means) and hit it big on the small screen in smaller roles in the following years. He is arguably best remembered for his iconic presence on television shows as a guest star, notably *All in the Family*, in which he kissed lovable bigot Archie Bunker smack dab on the lips.

We'd also like to mention his wonderful yet unnecessary cameo in the 1980s dictator switcheroo comedy *Moon over Parador*, which starred Richard Dreyfuss in a dual mustache role, and the 1989 film *Tap*, which he starred opposite fellow tap-dancing 'stache brother Gregory Hines. His character in that film was called Little Mo, but there was nothing little about Davis's "mo-ustache."

While it wasn't exactly bursting at the seams like Geezer Butler's heavy-hitting mustache with Black Sabbath, Davis's mustache appeared nice and compact, sort of like an unraveled Brillo pad but a lot less rigid.

'Stache-o-Meter Rating

Sammy Davis Jr., like way too many legends, passed away long before he should've. That said, we'll remember the man, his music, and the decades he entertained us with a mustache more theatrical than a Celine Dion fist thump to the chest. For that, he gets a 7.5 on the 'Stache-o-Meter. In a rare exception to the rule, whatever happened in Vegas for Davis, didn't stay in Vegas. Thankfully, it stayed firmly under his nose.

TOP ELEVEN
OCEAN'S MUSTACHES

1. ELLIOTT GOULD, *BUSTIN'*

2. CESAR ROMERO, *THE DEVIL IS A WOMAN*

3. DON CHEADLE, *TALK TO ME*

4. WAYNE NEWTON, *THE ADVENTURES OF FORD FAIRLANE*

5. CASEY AFFLECK, *OCEAN'S 12*

6. MATT DAMON, *THE INFORMER*

7. AL PACINO, *DICK TRACY*

8. BERNIE MAC, *SOUL MEN*

9. SAMMY DAVIS JR., *MOON OVER PARADOR*

10. BRAD PITT, *INGLOURIOUS BASTERDS*

11. GEORGE CLOONEY, *MEN WHO STARE AT GOATS*

Ma-Ma-Mustache!

Stern may be the "King of All Media," Robin Quivers may pleasure herself with garden vegetables, and Artie Lange may be the "Lord of the Anal Ring Toss," but Gary Dell'Abate—as far as we're concerned—is the real reason why we listen to *The Howard Stern Show*. With a face for radio and a mouth that extends wider than that of the most flexible porn star, this horse-toothed jackass keeps order in a kangaroo court each morning and serves as the butt of many jokes.

While we admire the man behind the mic, we recall the better days when he used to have quite the mustache. Though "Bababooey" has been facial hair-free for the past decade or so, we remember those good old days when the renowned executive producer resembled New York Mets' slugger Keith Hernandez. Only instead of Gold-Glove skills and soap-opera star looks, he had a mullet, unearthly gums, and large teeth—and an amazing mustache to help cover up (or accentuate) his worst features! Yes, long before stories of a Jenna Jameson gangbang or tales of a Blue Iris Sybian ride, Dell'Abate rocked his Caucasian afro and mustache like they were going out of style. And sadly for us, they did.

'Stache-o-Meter Rating

If ever there was an upper-lip pube club (and we're pretty sure there was, and still is), we'd bet members would welcome Bababooey back with open arms—and in his case, gaping mouths. That retro mustache ranks 7.5 on the 'Stache-o-Meter. But it could have been higher than Crackhead Bob at a frat mixer if he didn't rid the world of his fuzz patch.

TOP FIVE MUSTACHED MEN WITH FACES FOR THE RADIO

1. DIETER ZETSCHE
2. CHARLES BRONSON
3. DANNY TREJO
4. DOUG HENNING
5. DON KING

Walt Disney

It's a Small 'Stache After All

Walter Elias Disney seemed to always want to dabble with the doodle. The Chicago-born storyteller, animator, producer, writer, and director broke into the animation business following stints as an ambulance driver in World War I and the American Red Cross Ambulance Force in France. After his first company went bankrupt, Disney traveled to Hollywood, where he found fame thanks to the mouse he drew named Mickey. He never looked back, and apparently never shaved the bristles off his face.

Steamboat Willie became the first cartoon with sound in 1928, and by the late 1930s and early 1940s, Disney was already a legend. *Snow White and the Seven Dwarfs*, *Dumbo*, and *Bambi* were just some of the studio's animated classics released during that period.

Cinderella, Peter Pan, and *Lady and the Tramp* followed in the 1950s. And in 1955, Walt opened Disneyland in California and—from what we understand—you had to be old enough to sport a 'stache to ride the *really* thrilling rides.

By the 1960s, Disney's imagination led to new Hollywood heights. *Mary Poppins* was a huge hit, combining live action with animation. *The Mickey Mouse Club* was also launched during that decade. However, on a sad note, Walt passed away from lung cancer at age 65 in '66.

Brother Roy O. Disney continued to build the Disney brand by opening Walt Disney World in Orlando, Florida, in 1971. He kept the company rolling each year thereafter. Thankfully, Walt wasn't alive to see Britney Spears on *The Mickey Mouse Club* or the 1995 release of *Pocahontas.* "Paint with all the colors of the wind"? Let's try writing a plot first.

'Stache-o-Meter Rating

Walt Disney will always be remembered for bringing smiles to children's faces, and, of course, the perfectly shaped line of hair growing between his nose and top lip. The creator of such classics as *Fantasia* and *Pinocchio* had one Magic Kingdom of a 'bert. It combined former CNN anchor Bernard Shaw's 'stache (only better groomed) with the similar one of lame comedian Sinbad. Overall, Disney's fuzz-above is a highly sought-after masterpiece—much like a VHS copy of *Cinderella* in the '90s—ranking an 8.5 on the 'Stache-o-Meter. Like the auteur himself, Disney's mustache is frozen in time.

TOP FIVE GREAT 'STACHED DISNEY CHARACTERS

1. ROY DISNEY
2. SHAN YU, *MULAN*
3. GEPETTO, *PINNOCHIO*
4. THE RINGMASTER, *DUMBO*
5. CAPTAIN HOOK, *PETER PAN*

TOP TEN TOONS WITH MUSTACHES

1. MURKY DISMAL, *RAINBOW BRITE*
2. CLEVELAND BROWN, *FAMILY GUY*
3. MAN-AT-ARMS, *HE-MAN AND THE MASTERS OF THE UNIVERSE*
4. YOSEMITE SAM, *LOONEY TUNES*
5. NED FLANDERS, *THE SIMPSONS*
6. MR. SPACELY, *THE JETSONS*
7. SNIDELY WHIPLASH, *DUDLEY DO-RIGHT*
8. PURPLE PIE MAN, *STRAWBERRY SHORTCAKE*
9. PROFESSOR HINKLE, *FROSTY THE SNOWMAN*
10. SPIKE, *PEANUTS*

The Vince Lombardi of Mustaches

Gridiron great Mike Ditka is the only man in Chicago Bears history to have won a championship as a player and as a head coach. A star on the field as well as the sidelines, his mustache was right smack in the middle of the action. Well, as a coach anyway.

For six years (1961–1966), a clean-shaven Iron Mike made a name for himself in the Windy City playing tight end but never being much of a tight ass. Rather than going into the lame duck later seasons of his playing career (the Philadelphia Eagles and Dallas Cowboys), we'll jump to the year 1982, a year in which Boy George pranced around in a dress, but more importantly, Ditka scored big as a coach.

Ditka earned a reputation as a gutsy warrior and unorthodox leader—perhaps best known for snubbing Hall-of-Famer Walter Payton in SuperBowl XX when he opted to go with fellow bert-wearing Bear William "The Fridge" Perry for the one-yard touch-down run.

Speaking of facial-haired fridges, Ditka had the most docu-mented mustache in NFL history. No fumble here, the Ditkastache is as classic as the prestigious career the Hall-of-Famer put together, leaving absolutely no trace of flesh from roughly his left-to-right cheeks. This outspoken mustache warranted its own highlight reel or halftime show, and is worthy of an epic bio-flick like *We Are Marshall*. We'd cast a CGI-resurrected Captain Kangaroo–mustache to play the part.

Those famous whiskers not only earned the working-class hero praise among his peers (we hear Bob Costas sort of liked it), but also scored him a few endorsement deals, and most notably served as inspiration for the recurring *Saturday Night Live* skit "The Superfans," which featured a group of Chicago fans sporting self-adhesive mustaches. The pack was led by Norm from *Cheers*, who would never deliver another believable performance until years later when he starred in Michael Jackson's *Black & White* video.

Throughout the years, Ditka's career has taken him in and out of the sports world. He came out of semi-retirement to coach the New Orleans Saints, he served as a broadcaster on various NFL programs, and most recently costarred as himself in Will Ferrell's soccer would-be comedy *Kicking and Screaming*. Well, at least he kept his mustache intact and didn't show off his arse like Terry Brad-shaw did in *Failure to Launch*.

'Stache-o-Meter Rating

Mike Ditka inspired many pigskin heroes during his historic career. His work ethic inspired players, and his mustache paved the way for coaches like Dave Wanstedt, Andy Reid, Mike Holmgren, and Herm Edwards. For its perfect form and trendsetting ways, the Ditkastache earns a touchdown with a two-point conversion on the 'Stache-o-Meter 8. It features the best of vintage Dallas Cowboy Randy White's mustache with the worst of Dr. Phil's. We only deduct points for his participation in "SuperBowl Shuffle." (Looking at Jim McMahon rap is like visualizing Betty White naked: It ain't pretty but you sort of want to see it.)

TOP TEN GRIDIRON GREATS WITH GOLDEN MUSTACHES

1. LARRY CSONKA
2. DICK BUTKUS
3. MARK GASTINEAU
4. ANTHONY MUNOZ
5. BEN DAVIDSON
6. PHIL MCCONKEY
7. DAN DIERDORF
8. JEFF HOSTETLER
9. RANDY WHITE
10. WARREN MOON

The Thinking Man's Mustache

Albert Einstein is considered one of the greatest thinkers in the world. The theoretical physicist caught the world's attention and forever changed science with his often-controversial but always influential internationally recognized theories. Perhaps even more important than his contributions to that field was his underrated keen sense of style.

Next to Kurt Cobain, the German-born Jew and Swiss citizen was the only heterosexual man to pull off wearing a cardigan. His well-documented and often wrongly mocked pre–Don King hairstyle added more character to a man who already had his share of personality. Above all else, however, he was knowledgeable in *schnurrbart* etiquette. The nucleus of his face, this well-groomed mustache, fired up furry neutrons from one side of his face to the other.

Einstein never seemed to let his mustache get too out of control like his hairdo. It combined the Muppets' Swedish Chef with shades of folksinger Jim Croce's facial hair, and it was pure genius.

Speaking of genius, we can't forget the smarts behind the 'stache. Ironically, Einstein never completed high school and failed an entrance exam to a Swiss tech institute but would eventually come into his own working for the Swiss Patent Office. Before long, he was coming up with theories and writing renowned articles on things like Brownian motion, which dealt with molecular kinetic energy and had nothing to do with bowel movements as the name suggested.

A distinguished college professor who drew crowds all over the world, his general theory of relativity and infamous formula of the equivalence of mass and energy $E = mc^2$ also led to international fame. He would go on to win a Nobel prize for physics, and would continue to make important contributions that common folk like us could never quite fathom even if we tried. That's why we focus on the brilliant 'stache.

'Stache-o-Meter Rating

The term *genius* gets tossed around a lot, but Albert Einstein is one man who truly merits that distinction. It's no wonder *Time* magazine singled him out as their "Person of the Century" in 2000. But like we said, his mustache wasn't exactly chopped liver. Not quite the 'stache of the century but pretty darn close (it aces Mark Twain's thick mustache, which looked like a furry pickle clasped between his nose and upper lip), Einstein thinks his way up to a 9 on the 'Stache-o-Meter. It had mass, it had density, and it signified a quantum leap in mustache evolution.

Sam Elliott

Mamas, Don't Let Your Babies Grow Mustaches

Roy Rogers and Gene Autry may have put cowboys on the map, and John Wayne might be referred to as "The Duke," but there's only one cowboy we'd want on our frontier, and that's Sam Elliott. The legendary character actor might not have a fast-food chain named after him, an affliation with a California baseball team with identity issues, or a *True Grit* Oscar on his mantel, but he does have something all of the aforementioned legends don't have: a mustache of epic proportions. Full-bodied and rich in texture, Elliott's mustache, a live-action version of Captain Crunch's nasal support, has helped him remain a crucial supporting player in film and television for over three decades.

Elliott got his start by doing some stage work and guest-starring on such infamous television shows as *Hawaii Five-O* and *Mission: Impossible*. He made the leap to the big screen in the 1969 western *Butch Cassidy and the Sundance Kid*, and never really looked back. After making a string of flicks in the 1970s that focused on his body and rugged good looks (notably *Lifeguard* and *In the Legacy*), the actor came into his own playing gunslingers and frontiersmen. Standouts include Virgil Earp in *Tombstone*, General John Buford in *Gettysburg*, and Wild Bill Hickock in television's *Buffalo Girls*. But this cowboy isn't a one-trick pony. Some of his finest work has gone well beyond the cattle ranch. In particular, he garnered acclaim for his role as a good-natured biker in the 1985 Rocky Dennis bio-flick *Mask*, and became a legend on the college circuit by playing The Stranger/narrator in the Coens' cult classic *The Big Lebowski*. In recent years, Elliott has played a general in super-boring *Hulk*, a caretaker in the visibly uninspiring *Ghost Rider*, and a hero in the misdirected *Golden Compass*. And, for the most part, he's kept the mustache intact. (Although we still don't understand why he felt compelled to shave it off for the 1990s political thriller *The Contender*.)

'Stache-o-Meter Rating

Elliott played a cancer-riddled Marlboro Man in the 2005 comedy *Thank You for Smoking*. We'd like to take the time to thank Elliott for keeping his mustache on for all these years by awarding him our only 10 on the 'Stache-o-Meter—our apologies to Mr. Reynolds. Yes, throughout his career, he's been singled out for his acting, his physique, his rugged good looks, and raspy voice, but to us, his big and bushy mustache is—to quote Vince Vaughn's *Swingers* character—"money." That's some cold hard 'stache.

You Have the Right to Remain Hairy

On a historic *NYPD Blue* episode, the popular ABC drama's star, Dennis Franz, made headlines by dropping his clothes and his dignity and showing his ass in a key shower scene. While that "sweeps week" ploy drew big ratings, it was another anatomical feature of Detective Andy Sipowicz that had us watching each week. It was an arresting patch of fur on his face.

Yes, the actor may have shared scenes with a rotation of costars, from David Caruso to Jimmy Smits to that kid from *Silver Spoons*, but it was his mustache that gave the actor his finest support. It stood by Franz every time he was locking up thugs, interviewing perps, or tossing out racist barbs like they were going out of style.

Even better, the actor kept his mustache intact off the set and out of the precinct. Aside from a horrid miniseries starring Heather Locklear, *Texas Justice*, in which he shaved his signature 'stache, Franz let his mustache do the walking on and off camera throughout his career. From *Die Hard II* to *City of Angels* to the Emmy Awards—that in and of itself should earn the actor a badge of honor—he perpetually wore his mustache proudly above his lip.

'Stache-o-Meter Rating

Dennis Franz created one of the most memorable characters ever on network television; and through it all, he did it with fuzzy facial heaven. His mustache was a cross between Barney Miller's mustachioed likeness and Frida Kahlo's unibrow. For that, Dennis Franz earns an 8 on the 'Stache-o-Meter scale. We'll take the Sipowicz 'stache over the Sipowicz ass any day.

TOP FIVE
LAW-ABIDING MUSTACHES

1. *NYPD BLUE'S* DENNIS FRANZ

2. *MIKE HAMMER'S* STACY KEACH

3. *DAYS OF OUR LIVES'* JAMES REYNOLDS

4. *THE WARDEN'S* BRIAN DENNEHY

5. *NIGHT COURT'S* CHARLES ROBINSON

He Let His Mustache Do the Talking

Mohandas Karamchand Gandhi started out as a lawyer. But eventually he became a political and spiritual leader in India, long admired for protesting without the use of force. Gandhi took down an empire with his nonviolent practices and helped his country gain its independence from the British. Dubbed the "Father of the Nation," the activist was also known for showing a little more skin than other world leaders, and for abstaining from sex after he and his wife had kids.

Another constant for the leader, of course, was his mustache, which couldn't have been more evident against his bald head if it were written in Sanskrit. In addition, it's said that Gandhi took a vow of silence one day a week for reflection—something Sir Richard Attenborough should be doing every day since making the boring 1982 film about the great leader's life. The film may have been praised by the Academy of Motion Picture Arts and Sciences (it won, among other things, Best Picture, Best Actor for Ben Kingsley, and Best Director for Attenborough), but in our book, *E.T.* was robbed. Seriously, how many kids did you know who went around dressed up as Gandhi on Halloween?

'Stache-o-Meter Rating

After inspiring a nation, Gandhi was assassinated in 1948. But like so many great leaders, his beliefs and memory live on in all of us. So will his mustache, which was equal parts Theodore Roosevelt and old-school Walt "Clyde" Frazier. For that, Gandhi earns a 7.5 on the 'Stache-o-Meter. The Hindu may have had a small frame, but he wore that bert well.

TOP FIVE HISTORICAL FIGURES WITH MUSTACHES

1. EMPEROR HIROHITO

2. GANDHI

3. FRIEDRICH NIETZSCHE

4. JOSEF STALIN

5. THEODORE ROOSEVELT

Jason Giambi

Performance-Enhanced Mustache

Only one man can say he got the final hit in the "House That Ruth Built," and it's not Ken Phelps. (That ballplayer did, however, have a stirring mustache to match his then-iconic G.I. Joe Monkeywrench–style specs, but enough about that guy.) Jason Giambi's bloop single sent the Bronx out of Yankee Stadium in style in 2008, but even more so, the entire final season at the stadium was highlighted by his rugged mustache worthy of Monument Park.

That summer, Giambi needed to break out of his batting slump. He tried golden thongs, but growing a furry baseball bat under his nose ended up sending him on the right path. He busted out of his rut and even became the only player whose name is not Keith

Hernandez to garner a mustache giveaway night at a ballpark in his honor. But there's more to Giambi than a pinstriped push broom.

Born in West Covina, California, Giambi attended South Hills High School, where he made his mark in football, basketball, and obviously the national pastime. He played ball at Long Beach State, was drafted by the Oakland Athletics in 1992, and made his debut in the "bigs" in 1995. The first baseman/designated hitter made Oakland fans forget all about Mark McGwire, posting Silver Slugging seasons with the A's, and even earning an American League MVP with the team. The perennial all-star's Yankee career, which started in 2001, was mostly up then down but he failed to net any World Series rings in pinstripes. (Glennallen Hill has one by the way.) Still, the "Giambino," as John Sterling so annoyingly called him, went to the big dance in 2003 and has reached the playoffs each year except 2008. Not too shabby for Mr. Shaggy.

Let's focus on that final Yankee year again. Giambi rose above previous steroid-abuse charges with big numbers, and while the Yankees failed to reach October baseball, he provided a lot of pop and clubhouse leadership. That's saying a lot. It's hard to look Mattingly-tough when you're sharing first base duties with guys named Wilson Betemit and Shelley Duncan. But, it was Giambi's decision to grow some fuzz that will make him a Yankee legend now and for years to come. Most likely patterned from a Mike Pagliarulo mold with a dash of Claudell Washington and a third of Steve Balboni, Giambi's mustache always batted 1,000.

Whether it was dyed black or kept au naturel, his bert brought sort of an '80s nostalgia back to the game—days when stale bubblegum was commonplace within a wax pack of Topps instead of game-used jockstraps or what have you in them nowadays. His mustache swept the nation and reminded us of heroes from that

Jem and the Misfits decade like Mike Schmidt and Jim Rice. The '80s were all about blasting mammoth homeruns with mammoth mustaches, and Giambi was no different. If only he had focused on Gold Gloves instead of gold thongs, but that's another story.

'Stache-o-Meter Rating

Giambi's face grass is all natural and among the greatest fuzzy phenomena in the history of the national pastime, one that includes both the New York Metropolitans' "Sir" Timothy Keefe and St. Louis Cardinal Al "The Mad Hungarian" Hrabosky. Oh, and Alviro Espinosa, because that guy's mustache played errorless ball for over a decade. If there were a Cooperstown for mustaches, Giambi would be first ballot all the way. If only he'd grown it earlier. Because of that, he gets a 7 on the 'Stache-o-Meter. His 'stache is arguably the most historic event to happen in New York baseball history since the Yankees blew four games in a row during the 2004 ALCS and Phil Rizzuto whored out the Money Store.

TOP FIVE MAJOR LEAGUE MASCOTS WITH MUSTACHES

1. BERNIE BREWER, MILWAUKEE BREWERS

2. LOU SEAL, SAN FRANCISCO GIANTS

3. TEDDY ROOSEVELT, WASHINGTON NATIONALS

4. DANDY, NEW YORK YANKEES

5. MR. REDLEGS, CINCINNATI REDS

Arsenio Hall

A Mustache That Made Us Go, Hmmm

Whether it was his brief stint as Buckwheat's bodyguard on *Saturday Night Live*, hosting his own popular talk show, pumping his fist in a Paula Abdul video, or appearing side-by-side with pal Eddie Murphy in the box office hit *Coming to America*, Arsenio Hall established himself in the late 1980s and early 1990s as the best thing to happen to America since Alf landed in Willie Tanner's garage.

The Cleveland native wasn't merely the Haim to Murphy's Feldman. He was a triple threat (actor-comedian-talk-show host), whose versatility knew no bounds. The same could be said for his mustache, which sparkled like Soul Glow. Hall's upper-lip paradise was never more prominent than while he was hosting *The Arsenio*

Hall Show, which ushered in an eclectic mix of new and established stars from 1989 to 1994.

While Hall will be best remembered for his series of dog pound "woo woos" and impressive guest list, it's his camera-friendly mustache that really stands out. Yes, that Solid Gold 'stache nearly upstaged that high-top fade and awkwardly padded suits every night.

In 1989, Arsenio released an album *Large and In Charge* under the guise of Chunky A., his overweight little brother. Some might say this move belongs on the career suicide shelf right next to Paul Reuben's trip to an adult-movie theater, but we give the man props for trying to gain some more street cred from the hip-hop community. Hey, Sugar Hill Gang sold records rapping about McDonald's. You can't blame the man.

'Stache-o-Meter Rating

So what if he didn't kick Jay Leno's ass, that he starred with an overweight Samoan (Sammo Hung) on a crappy television drama, or that he grew dreadlocks and became a second-rate Ed McMahon in the 2000s, Arsenio Hall stands out as a "large and in charge" talent. As far as his mustache, he nets a 7.5 on the 'Stache-o-Meter scale, losing points for shaving it off to play Semmi in *Coming to America*, but regaining form by playing fuzzy-faced preacher and "Sexual Chocolate" opening act Rev. Brown in that same comedy. Part Richard Pryor circa *Superman III* with a slight variation of late *Bébé's Kids'* founding father Robin Harris, we give Hall's mustache a big "woo woo" in the dog pound of mustaches.

TOP TEN
UNDERRATED MUSTACHES

1. *THE MUPPETS'* LEW ZEALAND

2. ARTIST FRIDA KAHLO

3. *MIKE TYSON'S PUNCH OUT'S* SODA POPINSKI

4. *SANFORD AND SON'S* DESMOND WILSON

5. *BATMAN'S* ALAN NAPIER

6. *ROCKY I–VI'S* TONY "DUKE" BURTON

7. *THE PRINCESS BRIDE'S* MANDY PATINKIN

8. TAINTED TRACK STAR BEN JOHNSON

9. *WKRP IN CINCINNATI'S* HOWARD HESSEMAN

10. *M*A*S*H'S* MIKE FARRELL

MC Hammer

A Mustache 2 Legit 2 Quit

Cain versus Abel. David versus Goliath. Hulk versus Andre. Throughout our history, there have been some epic battles, but none bigger than the 1990 face-off between ego-boosting "rappers" Vanilla Ice and MC Hammer. In a time where the only rap music to go mainstream was that featuring lyrics about flashy kicks and favorite fast-food joints (mostly White Castle), these two icons went mano a mano, and as time has clearly shown us: They essentially both lost. But that's not the point. In the early 1990s, it was clearly "Hammer Time" all the time. Vanilla Ice jumped the shark when he rapped about Teenage Mutant Ninja Turtles.

Hammer rose to prominence in the late 1980s and early 1990s with his trademark baggy pants, lines shaved at his temples, Urkel glasses frames, and hit singles. The rapper had always played up his persona to be larger than life, but when it came to his MC mustache, it was understated—sort of like Prince meets Vincent Price by way of Nelly. Still, it worked, and was by far more gangsta than any of his PG to PG-13 lyrics.

Born Stanley Burrell, Hammer always seemed destined to be around mustaches. Raised in Oakland, he served as the Athletics' batboy for a while, offering tips to A's mustache bastions Reggie Jackson and Rollie Fingers. While he wanted to wear cleats and a cup, he failed to reach the big leagues and ultimately left the Bay Area for the navy. After getting discharged there, he focused on a career at the mic.

He started out recording Christian-inspired tunes, but not the cornball ones for which Amy Grant became famous. He debuted on rap charts with *Feel My Power*, an album that didn't heat up the charts like a Rick Astley tune, but did gain him attention. The album would lead to a record contract and a wide-scale rerelease under the name *Let's Get It Started*.

That album spawned hits like "Turn This Mutha Out," and paved the way for his biggest success: 1990's *Please Hammer Don't Hurt 'Em*. The first album to reach diamond status, it included hits like "U Can't Touch This," which sampled braided-mustache veteran Rick James's "Super Freak," and "Pray," which featured similarly 'stached Prince's "When Doves Cry" in the background.

While he was beloved by Casey Kasem, Hammer lost street cred with his clean-cut image. Lunch boxes and Barbie dolls in his likeness didn't help matters much, but made nice collectables for rich white kids. In 1991, Hammer's follow-up *Too Legit to Quit* went platinum, but his career took a turn for the worse when he wrote the theme song for *The Addams Family* movie. The accompanying video for that song is reportedly banned in heaven.

Ever since then, Hammer has tried to heat up the charts by releasing album after album (usually on a different label), but he's essentially gone the way of Peter Cetera after he made the "Glory of Love" video. He has become more infamous for filing for bankruptcy and getting torn new ones by gangsta rappers in their song lyrics.

In recent years, he's appeared on *The Surreal Life* on VH1, launched a dance website, and has become a successful preacher, but unfortunately for Hammer, everything he's touched since 1993 has pretty much turned into whatever the opposite of gold is. But, there is a silver lining for Hammer's legacy: While his music can be criticized, his mustache is bulletproof. Sure it's appeared and reappeared through his career, but overall, it's been the one constant in his career. Can't touch this? You're damn right we can't.

'Stache-o-Meter Rating

In an era when rappers spewed out lines about killing cops, banging bitches, and doing drugs in bathroom stalls, MC Hammer's routine was as pure as the cocaine Grandmaster Flash used to sing about. So was his mustache. Thin and authentic like a vintage Fiona Apple, Hammer nailed the 'stache and for that he scores a solid 7 on the 'Stache-o-Meter. In a class that included Ice-T's cornrows, Flava Flav's clock, and Humpty Hump's nose, Hammer's mustache was the best hip-hop accessory of the 1990s.

A RAPPER'S DELIGHT OF THE TOP FIVE OLD SCHOOL 'STACHES

1. FAB 5 FREDDY

2. KURTIS BLOW

3. SLICK RICK

4. CHRISTOPHER "PLAY" MARTIN

5. THE FRESH PRINCE

TOP TEN MUSTACHES EVEN HAMMER CAN'T TOUCH

1. JULIUS CARRY III, *THE LAST DRAGON*

2. MORGAN FREEMAN

3. OMAR SHARIF

4. BO DIDDLEY

5. OBBA BABATUNDE

6. JOSH BROLIN, *NO COUNTRY FOR OLD MEN*

7. RIP TAYLOR

8. LEMMY KILMINSTER, MOTORHEAD

9. ROBERT SHAW, *JAWS*

10. BURT LANCASTER, *JUDGMENT AT NUREMBERG*

Doug Henning

He Pulled a Mustache Out of His Face

David Blaine can starve himself and frolic upside down as much as he wants. David Copperfield can revel in making the Statue of Liberty disappear and creating the grandest illusion of them all by dating Claudia Schiffer in the 1990s. But if we had to select just one magician, Doug Henning would be the mightiest of all time. It has little to do with his actual magic, however, and everything to do with the fuzzy magic wand he had across his face. The illusionist was soft-spoken, but his mustache screamed "Abracadabra!"

Long before Henning arrived on the scene, magicians were argu-ably best known for capes, tuxes, and card tricks. Henning took the medium to a new level with his hippie getup: donning a magical bert, a Valerie Bertinelli–feathered do, flashy boots, and snug jumpsuit pants that left little to the imagination.

Before he became a worldwide sensation, Henning grew up in Winnipeg idolizing Harry Houdini and the art of illusion. After performing magic on a small scale, he soon became an international sensation by unveiling a theatrical magic show in Toronto called *Spellbound*. The show broke box office records and led to a Broadway incarnation simply called *The Magic Show*.

Henning and his over-the-top flamboyant magic act along with his Merlin-esque facial hair—not to mention his Freddy Mercury overbite—may have pulled off the greatest magic trick of them all in 1975 when 50 million captivated Americans tuned into his prime-time special *Doug Henning's World of Magic*. That show made us forget all about Houdini and his water torture escape tricks.

Throughout the 1970s and 1980s, Henning appeared alongside such iconic stars as Johnny Carson, Crystal Gale, Captain Kangaroo, and Miss Piggy. While his star faded a bit in the 1990s (he hung up his tights and tried political office at one point), the Canadian-born magician made even the simplest of tricks look like miracles. And let's face it, aside from that bag of tricks, his mustache made us all believe. That bushy 'stache was three-dimensional and never played any mind games. No optical illusion, Henning's hair was there in full effect, as if *Inspector Gadget*'s Chief Quimby's cartoon 'stache had magically come to life and then mated with *The Muppet*'s Swedish Chef's mustache.

'Stache-o-Meter Rating

Doug Henning did more with his bare hands on network television than Dennis Franz did with his bare ass. Speaking of bare asses, if only Henning had been around to help fellow illusionists Siegfried and Roy escape from their white Bengal tiger, Montecore. Speaking of hairy beasts, Henning's mustache was untamed. For that, he scores a 9.5 on the 'Stache-o-Meter. Even though Henning has sadly disappeared (way before his time), his mustache and memorable magic have given us all a feeling of wonder that no magician can ever make disappear.

TOP FIVE INCREDIBLY SHRINKING MUSTACHES

1. BOB DYLAN
2. NELLY
3. YOUNG MC
4. TERRENCE HOWARD
5. LOU BEGA

He's Keith Hernandez . . .

The bases are loaded in the bottom of the ninth inning, it's a full count, and in this high-stakes game of mustache supremacy there is only one logical choice of who should be up at the plate—Keith Hernandez. Yes, in a duel between 1980s New York first basemen with a flash of the glove and fuzziness, the man they call "Mex" trumps Don Mattingly any day of the week (off days, too). With eleven Gold Gloves, two World Series rings (one with the "Amazins"), and a mustache that knocked it out of the park even with the wind blowing in, Hernandez and his hairy upper lip were always the toast of the town. They still are.

Hernandez was born in San Francisco, but he left his heart there when he was drafted by the St. Louis Cardinals in 1971 as the 776th pick. The athlete would make his major league debut three years later for the same club in 1979, now drenched in full fuzzy mustache regalia; he led the National League with an impressive .344 batting average. Those stats earned him a piece of the Most Valuable Player Award with the Pirates' push broom legend Willie Stargell.

Hernandez would eventually lead the Redbirds into a World Series Championship matchup against Harvey's Wallbangers, better known as the Milwaukee Brewers. The significance of this particular Fall Classic was that it became the first ever meeting between Hernandez's perfectly combed Cardinals 'stache and Robin Yount's bushy Brew Crew bert. After seven games, the Hairy Hernandez caterpillar led the Cards to the promised land.

After coming to blows with general manager Whitey Herzog, Hernandez was traded to the New York Mets a year after winning baseball's top prize, for pitchers Neil Allen and Rick Ownbey (a.k.a. "Um, *who*?"). The only trade worse than this was when the New York Yankees traded stolen-base legend Rickey Henderson to the Oakland A's for Eric Plunk and a bag of nibs (the equivalent to Luis Polonia and his contributions to the game of baseball). With Hernandez now implanted at first base, the Metropolitans improved by twenty-two games in his first year in the Big Apple.

In 1986, the Miracle Mets had a mustache-riding (Hernandez, Wally Backman, Davey Johnson, Howard Johnson . . . we could go on) 108–54 record, and dramatically won the World Series against Bill Buckner, his bert, and his Boston Red Sox. The following year, the Gold Glove God was named the first captain in team history. One would imagine Rusty Staub cried that day.

By the end of the 1989 season, after suffering some nagging injuries, Hernandez signed with the Cleveland Indians. Sadly for Hernandez, this was no Hollywood script where a hobbled Tom Berringer would beat out an infield flatulent to win the pennant. Unfortunately after just forty-three games, the two-time champion had taken his last licks.

Two years after hanging up his cleats, Hernandez appeared as himself in a two-part episode of *Seinfeld*. The Jerry bro-mance matched with a JFK "lone gunman" theory subplot aside, Hernandez's appearance on the show was the greatest thing to happen to sitcom television since the arrival of Kirk Cameron BFF, Boner Stabone.

These days, the whiskered World Series warrior is working the tube as a baseball analyst for his beloved Mets on the SNY television network. While his mustache is now a bit more pepper and salt (ironic since he promotes Just For Men with Walt "Clyde" Frazier), it's remained a constant on the man's face ever since the 1970s. This furry Louisville Slugger under his nose always bats 1,000 and always looks primed and ready for a *GQ* cover shot.

'Stache-o-Meter Rating

Easily the greatest defensive first baseman in Major League Baseball history, Keith Hernandez belongs in the Hall of Fame. While his chances seem nil, it'd be nice if Bud Selig stopped ruining real traditions of the game and considered opening a Mustache Appreciation Wing in Cooperstown. If so, Hernandez's mustache would be bronzed and placed on display. Combining the hairy essentials of *Sopranos* chef Artie Bucco's bert with the firmness of original American Gladiator Gemini, Hernandez's 'stache is the real field of dreams. For that, his garden grows to a solid 9 on the 'Stache-o-Meter.

Mustache-a-Mania Running Wild

Terry Bollea admittedly grew up a chubby kid. He was often picked last in sports. In between wedgies and warming the bench, he developed aspirations of becoming a rock star. So much for that. Little did he know that serving as a bouncer at local watering holes would eventually pave his way into the wrestling world.

Like many wrestlers, Bollea had to pay his dues in the business, enduring years of training and bad gimmicks as "Sterling Golden" or "Terry Boulder." It wasn't until he landed a role in *Rocky III* that Bollea, at that point known as Hulk Hogan, fully reached his potential. The character of "Ultimate Male" Thunderlips in Stallone's 1982 hit sequel brought Hogan worldwide exposure, his very first action figure, and—before long—wrestling gold.

On January 23, 1984, in front of a packed Madison Square Garden crowd, Hogan defeated fellow bert brethren the Iron Sheik for the World Wrestling Federation (now WWE) Heavyweight Championship. Winning the belt would catapult him from being simply another wrestler to a worldwide phenomenon.

"Hulkamania" ran wild in the 1980s, 1990s, and even today. Dolls were made in his likeness. "Hulkster" foam fingers and apparel were sold at every sold-out arena. He even inspired a Saturday morning cartoon show, which featured fellow grapplers Nikolai Volkoff and Junkyard Dog, but not Brutus Beefcake.

Hogan became the first (and only) wrestler to appear on a *Sports Illustrated* cover; he made appearances on *The Tonight Show* with Johnny Carson and *Saturday Night Live*; and he even shared the ring with Mr. T. and an unusual pop star known as Cyndi Lauper.

In the ring, Hogan accomplished unthinkable feats. He headlined eight of the first nine Wrestlemanias, the Super Bowl of professional wrestling. He won the WWF, WWE, and the World Championship Wrestling (WCW) Heavyweight Belts six times each. His match at Detroit's Pontiac Silverdome during Wrestlemania III—where he defeated Andre the Giant before a crowd of more than 90,000 fans—was arguably his best and most famous match. But, nothing can compare to the powerful rendition of Little Richard's "Tutti Frutti," which he performed with commentator "Mean" Gene Okerlund. Didn't he have a mustache, too?

Indeed, thanks to the Hulkster's appeal, in and out of the ring, kids wanted to be just like him. They wanted those "twenty-four-inch pythons" just like their hero. So they whipped up a grotesque protein shake that probably only made them have to go to the bathroom. That said, beyond the bandana; mustard-yellow tights; and the red, white, and blue, there was a golden handlebar mustache sitting right above his immortal lip. Yes, Captain Lou Albano's facial rubber bands had nothing on "the Hulkster"—who trained, said his prayers, took his vitamins, and grew one hell of a bleached-blond bert, brother.

'Stache-o-Meter Rating

It's true that Hogan made a string of really bad movies when he wasn't wrestling. He was involved in a steroid scandal, and even shaved off his mustache for a mediocre syndicated show, *Thunder in Paradise*. But all is forgiven. Because through it all, for the most part, he kept his bert intact—even when he decided to paint on a black beard as a founding member of the infamous New World Order (NWO) in WCW. Hogan's mustache—a mix of Martin Mull and the leather aficionado from the Village People—is just as big a trademark as the immortal leg drop. "A Real American" with a really great mustache, Hogan ranks a solid 8 on our 'Stache-o-Meter. Who would've thought that a fat kid from Tampa would become such a mega-power?

TOP FIVE
BODY-SLAMMIN' BERTS

1. HULK HOGAN
2. "RAVISHING" RICK RUDE
3. THE IRON SHEIK
4. HOWARD FINKEL
5. LANNY POFFO

TOP X WONDERFUL
WRESTLEMANIA WHISKERS

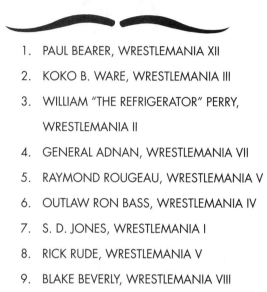

1. PAUL BEARER, WRESTLEMANIA XII

2. KOKO B. WARE, WRESTLEMANIA III

3. WILLIAM "THE REFRIGERATOR" PERRY,

    WRESTLEMANIA II

4. GENERAL ADNAN, WRESTLEMANIA VII

5. RAYMOND ROUGEAU, WRESTLEMANIA V

6. OUTLAW RON BASS, WRESTLEMANIA IV

7. S. D. JONES, WRESTLEMANIA I

8. RICK RUDE, WRESTLEMANIA V

9. BLAKE BEVERLY, WRESTLEMANIA VIII

10. SGT. SLAUGHTER, WRESTLEMANIA VII

Frida Kahlo

Mustaches . . . Not Just for Men

Throughout history, a great many women, from Gloria Steinem to Hillary Clinton to RuPaul, have stood up for female rights and have been an integral part of ensuring equality for all, no matter what gender. Somewhere along the way, however, one lady's most famous work was written out of the history books. Sure her artwork has been praised, and Salma Hayek even flashed her boobs in an acclaimed movie on her life, but Frida Kahlo achieved something that no one ever gives her credit for: She made mustaches on women cool. (Unibrows, too, but we're not about to write a book on that.)

To say the Mexican painter led a tragic life would be an understatement, like saying the Kennedy family experienced nothing but good times outside of Hyannis. Early on in her life, she survived a bout of polio and was seriously injured in a bus accident, injuries that plagued her her whole life. As she dealt with the pain, she dabbled with painting—her pictures were mostly self-portraits—and romanced acclaimed Mexican muralist Diego Rivera. That guy was much older than she was and couldn't keep it in his pants around other ladies. The pair married and divorced and then married again, and all the while Kahlo battled poor health but continued to paint. Her work eventually got her noticed, but it really wasn't truly appreciated until after she died.

All her life, Kahlo battled with something, be it infidelity, reportedly her sexuality, or the bus-accident injuries that caused her to have at least thirty operations. One thing, however, came naturally to her and caused her little discomfort. It was Kahlo's mustache, and it brightened up an often sad face, whether it was in person or on a canvas. And at the very least, it brought us joy, much like her paintings. Her face-mane was reminiscent of the prepubescent 'staches most of the original members of '80s sensation New Edition sported on their faces. But in her case, that was a good thing.

While it wasn't as prominent as, say, fellow Mexican Carlos Santana's "black magic" caterpillar, Kahlo's 'stache stands out in a league of its own. Boys will be boys, but mustaches will be mustaches, no matter what gender it is.

'Stache-o-Meter Rating

Kahlo sported a unibrow that if placed a on man's face would make quite a lovely mustache. But while her eye 'stache was something to behold, it was her mustache that was a true masterpiece. However, since women are equal to men, we won't grade Kahlo on a curve. She receives a 7 on the 'Stache-o-Meter because, let's face it, while the mustache is impressive for a woman, it'd be a weak-ass bert on any man.

TOP FIVE
SOUTH-OF-THE-BORDER 'STACHES

1. VICENTE FOX
2. DANNY TREJO
3. CHEECH MARIN
4. CARLOS SANTANA
5. FRIDA KAHLO

Captain Kangaroo

"Good Morning, Mustache!"

More cuddly than a Teddy Ruxpin and more impressive than Def Leppard's one-armed drummer, Bob Keeshan captivated children's imaginations for over fifty years as the lovably mustached and warmhearted Captain Kangaroo, becoming an iconic figure among millions of people around the world.

Before setting sail as captain of his kangaroo kingdom, Keeshan made his television debut in 1948 as the fun-loving Clarabell the Clown on the *Howdy Doody Show*. For four years Clarabell drove Buffalo Bob bonkers through various horn-honking schemes and practical jokes, eventually leading to a first-ballot unanimous entry into the Clown Hall of Fame in 1990. By the mid-'50s, as television networks began the search for new ways to approach children's programming, Keeshan and a pal came up with the concept for the *Captain Kangaroo* program. As the endearing lead character, Keeshan made the show an immediate success story. Along with big kangaroo-like pockets and even bigger bristles, every weekday the Captain would greet viewers with good-morning pleasantries and his prominent good-morning 'stache. Over the years countless stars dropped in, from the obnoxious and crazy Phyllis Diller to Bob Barker, Laverne and Shirley, an animated Charlie Brown, and of course Dolly Parton (every boy growing up in the '70s might remember her as the leading character in the story of that very first bulge in his pants).

Besides Keeshan's kangaroo gimmick, the show was a who's who of zany but educational characters who resided at the "Treasure House." Among the most memorable were Mr. Green Jeans (the Dyno-Mutt to the Captain's Blue Falcon—in other words his trusty sidekick), the Banana Man, puppets Bunny Rabbitt and Mr. Moose, and Bill Cosby right before he wore his very first Huxtable sweater. Of course, not every pitch by Kangaroo was hit out of the park. In fact, in 1980 the show debuted Slim Goodbody, a guy dressed in a body suit painted with internal organs. Sure the Goodbody body-stocking would make for a great Halloween costume these days, but for years it was arguably the most disturbing thing on television, perhaps only behind the Dudley molestation episode on *Diff'rent Strokes*.

'Stache-o-Meter Rating

Throughout all the magic drawing boards and Sweet Pickle Books, the Captain's flagship fuzz remained and earns him a 9 on the 'Stache-o-Meter. It will always be remembered and etched in our hearts as an American institution. So just what is Keeshan's recipe for mustache success? It's a half-teaspoon of Sonny Liston with a slight dash of *Popeye*'s Wimpy, and a full cup of former San Diego Padres manager Dick Williams. To make a comparison to another morning show back in the day, Keeshan had a "Magic Garden" under his nose.

TOP TEN LARGE AND IN CHARGE MUSTACHES

1. CAPTAIN KANGAROO

2. MAYOR DAVID DINKINS

3. LIEUTENANT MOSES HIGHTOWER

4. GENERAL THUNDERBOLT ROSS

5. CAPTAIN DARYL DRAGON

6. COMMISSIONER GORDON

7. INSPECTOR WALTER COBB

8. MANAGER BILLY MARTIN

9. CAPTAIN HOOK

10. COACH STAN VAN GUNDY

Don King

King of the Mustache Ring

Often imitated but never duplicated, for over thirty years Don King has been one of America's most well-known boxing promoters. Recognized best for his fork-in-a-socket highly outrageous hairstyle, over-the-top personality, and "main event" mustache, King has made his presence known in the boxing annals promoting some of the greatest names in the business, including Evander Holyfield and Roberto Duran.

After growing up in Cleveland and leading a rough-and-tough lifestyle, a young King—complete with his coif and mustache knockout combination—entered the boxing fray in the early 1970s, negotiating a highly anticipated heavyweight championship fight between "the greatest," Muhammad Ali, and a then-undefeated, pre-grilling George Foreman. While it was Ali who rope-a-doped his way past Foreman's mustache and scored the TKO, it was King who secured the then-record $10 million purse for the "Rumble in the Jungle."

King would later solidify his position as prizefighting's most prominent promoter by arranging a third and final showdown between Ali and his archrival, "Smokin'" Joe Frazier. This classic encounter was billed as the "Thrilla in Manila," but the real "Thrilla" was right under King's nose. (More on that knockout in a bit.)

King would spend most of the '70s and '80s building his empire, which included pound-for-pound the greatest collection of boxers in the world, notably Mike Tyson before and after he allegedly tossed *Head of the Class*'s Robin Givens into the wall of their apartment. Some of the pugilistic-whiskered warriors that have appeared under the Don King Promotions banner include Wilfredo "Bazooka" Gomez, Alexis Arguello, Azumah Nelson, and Aaron "The Hawk" Pryor.

Most of King's men had hall-of-fame credentials, while he had a mustache that should be enshrined somewhere. While it's more of a 1990s than a 1970s Sherman Hemsley mustache than we would've liked, there's no denying King's royal face broom is as appealing as those Everlast belts were back in the 1980s. Seriously, everyone had one of those.

'Stache-o-Meter Rating

Don King has had his fair share of controversy through-out his illustrious career. But despite accusations of tax evasion and jury-tampering, and lawsuits from former boxers, he's always managed to live the American dream. A prominent figure in American pop culture, King appro-priately coined the phrase "Only in America," and "Only in America" can a guy with such an awful haircut and only slightly better mustache than human punching bag Tim Witherspoon become a huge household name. For that alone, King KOs his way to a 7 on the 'Stache-o-Meter.

TOP TEN
KNOCKOUT MUSTACHES

1. JOHN L. SULLIVAN
2. BOBBY CZYZ
3. BARRY MCGUIGAN
4. ALEXIS ARGUELLO
5. SONNY LISTON
6. SUGAR RAY ROBINSON
7. REFEREE RICHARD STEELE
8. BALD BULL
9. PINKLON THOMAS
10. KEN NORTON

Ted Lange

Some Smooth 'Stache Sailing

Ted Lange's mustache wasn't exactly "exciting and new" on *The Love Boat*, but it was quite refreshing, considering the show mostly featured Charo rambling and dancing uncontrollably and the captain's daughter Julie roaming around like a lost and irritating puppy.

On a ship full of schmaltz, Lange's bartender Isaac was the cool that kept the cruise afloat. While he's best known for serving mai tais to Tom Bosley and Virgin Coladas to Carol Channing (we hope), Lange put together an impressive career that extended well beyond the *Pacific Princess* and Lou Gossett Jr. mustache.

Born in Oakland, Lange set off to become an actor early on by attending the Royal Academy of Dramatic Art. After connecting with audiences on the stage (he was fittingly in the show *Hair*), he popped up in several films including *Trick Baby*, where he played a memorable pimp named Melvin.

But Lange's calling came on the small screen, where he not only appeared but also wrote at times. After landing a gig playing Junior opposite Teddy Wilson's mustache on *That's My Mama*, the actor hit it big by growing what would best be described as an African Americanized Stacy Keach mustache in 1977 as Isaac the bartender on *The Love Boat*. The actor is still synonymous with that character, having played him in sequels and TV movie spin-offs, but he's found success away from the tacky tuxedo by guest-starring on such shows as *227*, a series where sassy Jackée was long overshadowed by Hal Williams's working-class 'stache, and *The King of Queens*, a critically acclaimed comedy, where Jerry Stiller's mustache upstaged Kevin James on any given night.

Lange has also thrived behind the scenes, directing television episodes and writing and directing acclaimed plays that have gone on to win prestigious awards.

That said, there's no question Lange will always be remembered as Isaac, and we'd imagine, that's just fine with him. Next to the Fonz and arguably Schneider from *One Day at a Time*, there wasn't a cooler character on 1970s TV sets than Lange's cruise liner drink specialist—and to think he did it all with a bowtie. Lange's mustache was an ounce of Southern Comfort that no doubt set sail in many ladies' cabins and quite possibly in Gopher's.

'Stache-o-Meter Rating

7.5

Ted Lange's mustache put the love in *Love Boat*. To take it a step further, we'd be so bold as to say it not only influenced Denzel Washington's *St. Elsewhere* hospital-drama bert as well as *The Office*'s Stanley's stationary 'stache, but if Salt n Pepa had been around back in the 1970s, it would possibly have made them want to "Shoop." For its shaken and stirred dexterity, Lange's upper-lip Afro travels up to a Stubing-approving 7.5 on the 'Stache-o-Meter. All aboard!

TOP TEN SMALL-SCREEN STARS WITH BIG-SCREEN 'STACHES

1. FATHER GUIDO SARDUCCI

2. *THE LOVE BOAT*'S TED LANGE

3. *MY NAME IS EARL*'S JASON LEE

4. *227*'S HAL WILLIAMS

5. *MONK*'S TED LEVINE

6. *CHICO AND THE MAN*'S FREDDIE PRINZE

7. *DEADWOOD*'S IAN MCSHANE

8. *20/20*'S JOHN STOSSEL

9. *HAPPY DAYS*' PAT MORITA

10. *CAGNEY & LACEY*'S JOHN KARLEN

Jason Lee

The Mustached Duke of *Earl*

If Bruce Lee is the master of martial arts, then Jason Lee is the master of the mustache. Whereas "The Dragon" became a legend for his fists of fury and roundhouse kicks, the former pro skateboarder and *My Name Is Earl* actor rocketed to fame by doing kickflips and ushering in a new era of whisker wearers.

Born and raised in Southern California, Lee dropped out of high school in his early teens to become a skateboarder. He eventually went pro, landed his own shoe deal, and started his own skateboarding company. While he became infamous on the Tony Hawk circuit, the acting bug stung him harder than a Rue McClanahan roll in the hay on *The Golden Girls*.

Lee's acting career went into overdrive in 1995 with the help of a bearded, chubby fanboy named Kevin Smith, who cast him in the lead role of Brodie Bruce in the crude classic *Mall Rats*. In 1997, Lee won an Independent Spirit Award for playing a comic book inker possibly in love with Ben Affleck in Smith's *Chasing Amy*. While that film role is arguably his career best, the actor has continued to work with Smith on such films as *Dogma*, *Jay and Silent Bob Strike Back*, and most recently, the turd of a sequel *Clerks II*.

Lee established himself well in the film industry with other films like *The Incredibles*, in which he voiced the villain, and Cameron Crowe's *Almost Famous*, where he played a member of the fictional 1970s group Stillwater (Billy Crudup's 'stache is a "Golden God" by the way). He also memorably starred in Crowe's *Vanilla Sky*, in which he played best bud to a disfigured pre–couch jumping Tom Cruise, and recently appeared in the live-action *Alvin and the Chipmunks*, which gnawed at the box office's and many a filmgoer's souls.

But Lee has arguably found most success on the boob tube (and that's not a Jaime Pressley reference). Since it debuted in 2005, *My Name Is Earl* has been a mainstay on NBC's Thursday night lineup. The series finds the actor sporting the best push broom on television since, arguably, Edward James Olmos's on *Miami Vice* (sorry Dennis Franz). Playing Earl Hicky, Lee is a lovable loser who wins the lottery, loses it, and realizes he needs to right all the wrongs in his life in order to change his karma.

At a time when mustaches weren't as trendy as they are nowadays (thanks emo-hipsters), Lee decided to grow a thick, almost gelatinous, mustache to add depth to his character.

He grew it for his role, not to make a statement. It's just there, and it's, as Will Ferrell playing James Lipton might say, "scrumtrulescent."

'Stache-o-Meter Rating

In Hinduism and Buddhism, karma essentially means your actions in this life will affect your next. If there is such a thing as reincarnation, we're confident Lee will be brought back as a hearty lion. The mane under his nose, sort of an homage to Bruce McGill's Sheriff Dean Farley mustache in *My Cousin Vinny*, roars louder than the MGM insignia ever could. A tribute to 1970s cops everywhere, the Earl fuzziness ranks a 9 on the 'Stache-o-Meter.

TOP FIVE MODERN TV MUSTACHES

1. MICHAEL IMPERIOLI, *LIFE ON MARS*

2. GRANT SHOW, *SWINGTOWN*

3. LESLIE DAVID BAKER, *THE OFFICE*

4. JIMMY SMITS, *DEXTER*

5. JAY JOHNSTON, *THE SARAH SILVERMAN PROGRAM*

Stan Lee

'Nuff 'Stache

More incredible than the Hulk, mightier than Thor, and yes, it's even more fantastic than any of the Fantastic Four, since the first appearance of your friendly neighborhood Spider-Man, Stan Lee and his amazing mustache have been a major contributor to the comic book world.

Born and raised in New York City, Stanley Lieber (perhaps his secret identity?) didn't rely on gamma rays or spider bites to gain superhero notoriety: With the help of a few friends (artists Steve Ditko and Jack Kirby) Stan Lee helped transform Marvel Comics from a small section of a publishing house to a worldwide multimedia corporation. (Let's give him a mulligan on that *Daredevil* movie, okay?)

Before putting Marvel on the map, Lee began his literary career writing obituaries and press releases until his work as a text filler for *Captain America* got him published in 1941. At nineteen, he became editor-in-chief of Marvel until 1972, when he became publisher of the company that introduced us to a full assortment of superheroes ranging from Alpha Flight and Power Pack to the mustachioed Dr. Strange and a seldom-used character named Charlie 27.

During the 1950s, as DC Comics was flying high with Superman and the Justice League among others, Lee and artist Jack Kirby created the Fantastic Four. The hugely popular success of the group led to a sudden rise in comic book popularity, which eventually paved the way for some of Marvel's mightiest to debut. Along with Kirby, he created Iron Man, Thor, Hulk, and the X-Men, and with help from Steve Ditko, he gave us Spider-Man and, among the most important for the purposes of this book, J. Jonah Jameson (Peter Parker's mustached editor-in-chief).

With the huge success of these and several other non-Lee-influenced superheroes (including those under the now defunct Dead Cricket Comics banner), he has become not only a public figure for Marvel but for the entire comic book universe, far more recognizable than both Pip the Troll and the lamest *X-Men* character ever, Lucas Bishop.

These days, Lee and his greatest superpowered creation (his mustache) spend most of their time dropping by various Comic Conventions across America and appearing in several of Marvel's biggest blockbuster movies of the past few years, including all three *Spider-Man* flicks, *Daredevil* (a.k.a. Ben Affleck's pre-*Gigli* crapper), and, of course, his riveting portrayal as Baxter Building's whiskered mailman Willie Lumpkin in *The Fantastic Four*.

Whether on or behind the scenes, Lee has always sported a super 'stache. To quote Jessica Rabbit—one sexy cartoon character that Lee had nothing to do with—his 'stache isn't "bad, it's just drawn that way."

'Stache-o-Meter Rating

The Stan Lee mustache speaks louder than the Inhuman's Blackbolt, combining the best traits of Gene Hackman's *Royal Tenenbaums* 'stache with the texture and toughness of "Mr. Blue," Edward Bunker. Some might wonder if Lee's facial fury was the inspiration behind X-Men fur ball, the Beast. We're not sure, but we do know this comic genius and his hairy little lip-mutant score an uncanny 7 on the 'Stache-o-Meter.

TOP FIVE MUSTACHES
IN THE MARVEL UNIVERSE

1. STAN LEE
2. TEXAS TWISTER
3. DR. STRANGE
4. THE LEADER
5. LOCKJAW

Bert in East L.A.

Richard "Cheech" Marin reportedly earned his nickname through his love of the Chicano food cheecharone. His mustache is more appetizing.

Born in East Los Angeles, Marin's worldwide recognition began in the 1970s as one half of one of the most successful comedy duos of all time—alongside greats like Kramden and Norton, Burns and Allen, and of course, television's *Bosom Buddies* Tom Hanks and Peter Scolari. After fleeing the United States at the height of the Vietnam War, he moved to Canada (home of the underrated Rick Moranis and John Candy, the latter of which had a mustache in *Planes, Trains, and Automobiles*) where he met his tag team partner Tommy Chong.

For over fifteen years, Cheech and Chong released outlandish marijuana-induced comedy albums such as *Big Bambu*, *Get Out of My Room*, and *Los Cochinos*, the last of which was highlighted by George Harrison playing guitar on the song "Basketball Jones." (No word if Sir George had a mustache in the studio.) The success of their albums quickly translated to instant film stardom with hits like *Up in Smoke* and *Nice Dreams*, which highlighted the duo's comedic styling, impeccable timing, and love for bong hits and women with big jugs. After years of ruling Southern California before "Fernando-mania" rolled into town, the two went their separate ways due to creative differences. Since the split, Chong has fallen on hard times (his daughter Rae Dawn would embarrass his namesake by appearing in the movie *Soul Man* and Chong himself would later serve time for getting busted for selling glass pipes), while Marin's career has been on a high. Marin, whose Mexistache has since gone "up in smoke," resurfaced as smooth-faced Inspector Joe Dominguez on the television show *Nash Bridges* opposite *Miami Vice* heartthrob Don Johnson and *Baywatch* backwash Yasmine Bleeth. He has enjoyed supporting roles in films like *Tin Cup*, *Desperado*, *From Dusk Till Dawn*, and the entire *Spy Kids* trilogy. His acclaimed voice-over work has included *Oliver and Company*, *The Lion King*, and most recently *Cars*.

In the spring of 2007, Marin cameoed in Quentin Tarantino and Robert Rodriguez's *Grindhouse*, portraying Padre Benicio Del Toro in *Machete* with fellow fittingly enough mustachioed Mexican American Danny Trejo. (We won't bother to get into his mustache-free and odd hair color job as Hugo's dad on *Lost*.)

'Stache-o-Meter Rating

No one can get over Cheech and Chong breaking up, but the real tragedy has been the separation of Cheech's face from his mustache. That mustache, a thick combination of Russian filmmaker Andrei Tarkovsky's and Al Sharpton's mustache, was sheer perfection in the 1970s, and had he left it intact, it would have received a solid 10 on the 'Stache-o-Meter. Instead, Marin has chosen to leave his trademark off his face, and for that he takes a "bong rip" and finishes at a disappointing 6.5. Put that in your 'stache pipe and smoke it!

TOP FIVE ALLEGED DRUG ABUSERS WITH 'STACHES

1. CHEECH MARIN
2. JAKE "THE SNAKE" ROBERTS
3. BARRY BONDS
4. JIMI HENDRIX
5. PAT O'BRIEN

The Mustache on Ice

Much like Canada occupies the majority of North America, a mustache occupies the majority of Lanny McDonald's face. For sixteen seasons, this Canadian legend has undoubtedly left his mark on the world of hockey. The right winger with the right whiskers played for the Toronto Maple Leafs, the Colorado Avalanche, and the Calgary Flames throughout his career in the National Hockey League.

The hard-hitting forward was the fourth overall pick in 1974 by Toronto, but his heart and his oversized red 'stache truly belong to the fans of Calgary. With his Yosemite Sam–inspired 'stache,

McDonald captured the City of Calgary by storm when he led the team to its first and only Stanley Cup Championship in 1989. As team leader, McDonald's memorable overtime goal in a 1978 Maple Leafs playoff game, scored despite a fractured wrist and broken nose, is a great example of what defined his hall-of-fame career and tough-guy persona.

The gritty Canadian was a tough leader who played with his heart on his sleeve every time he laced up his skates and combed his mustache. The only thing remotely tougher back in those days was Colt Seavers diving out of his *Fall Guy* pickup truck on a weekly basis.

In 1983, considered to be his best year on the ice, McDonald and his famous frozen fuzz battled Wayne Gretzky for top scoring rights as he poured in a career-high sixty-six goals and ninety-eight points. In 1989, his final season, McDonald was named hockey's Man of the Year, scoring his five-hundredth goal and thousandth point (a stat that adds goals scored with assists made). Shortly after hanging up his skates for good at the conclusion of the Flames' memorable Stanley Cup run the same year, McDonald became vice president of the team, and served in that capacity for several years; he also served as general manager for the Canadian national team.

Through his work over the years with many charitable organizations, McDonald truly deserves recognition as a high-class star with high-class 'stache. In a world of whiskered hockey personalities such as broadcaster Bill Clement, former Winnipeg Jet Dave Babych, and Jacques Grande (a fictional character played by Justin Timberlake in the not-so-laughable *Love Guru*), the McDonald mustache is the Wayne Gretzky of frozen facial fur. With the power play right under his nose, Lanny's hairy lip puck truly is the greatest show on ice.

'Stache-o-Meter Rating

Awarded the Bill Masterton Memorial Trophy for his dedication to hockey, Lanny McDonald should also earn praise for dedication to his nostril nest. His mustache combines the true essence of Sparky Lyle's bert with the cartoonish goodness of Woody Woodpecker arch-nemesis Wally Walrus, and for that, McDonald earns a flaming 9 on the 'Stache-o-Meter.

TOP FIVE HAIRIEST LIPS
IN HOCKEY HISTORY

1. LANNY MCDONALD

2. DENIS MARUK

3. ROGIE VACHON

4. TERRY RUSKOWSKI

5. BRYAN TROTTIER

All Hail the Queen . . . of Mustaches

With fist-pumping, timeless anthem-rock songs like "We Are the Champions" and "We Will Rock You," ditties like "Crazy Little Thing Called Love," and the opera-inspired classic "Bohemian Rhapsody," Freddie Mercury led the British group Queen to the top of the charts over a three-decade span.

The rock god, who was born on the island of Zanzibar before moving with his family to the U.K., served up infectious charisma, powerhouse vocals, and an energy that knew no bounds. Whether it was flamboyantly parading around stage, placing a microphone under his belt, or strutting around in skintight pants, the buoyant singer had audiences on their feet. One performance in particular,

1985's Live Aid at London's Wembley Stadium, was the defining moment in an already stellar career. Not only did the band upstage dozens of other artists that night, but it also put the spotlight on a big piece of royalty . . . mustache royalty that is.

Up until that gig, Mercury more or less led the group with a mullet and eyeliner. It wasn't until Live Aid, however, that he really established himself as a man with some serious 'stache. The front man's mustache wasn't quite as thick as another favorite Freddie of ours (Nietzsche) but it certainly did stick out—although not as much as the bulge he created in his pants. Combining traits of an always reliably well-groomed Uncle Leo 'stache from *Seinfeld* with a little Caucasian Lionel Richie flavor, Mercury's mustache simply fit the singer's face to a T. At the very least, it suited him better than Brian May's hairdo, which for some odd reason, has always looked like a Richard Simmons afro explosion.

Although he passed away well before his time, supplied songs to an overly hyped Christopher Lambert movie, and ended up not really liking "Fat Bottomed Girls" (or any girls for that matter), Mercury will always be remembered for his showmanship, his talent, and his bloody beautiful mustache.

'Stache-o-Meter Rating

Paul Rodgers may prance around stage now as a member of the legendary rock band Queen, but everyone knows only one name defines that rock super group: Freddie Mercury. And there was only one facial feature that defined the singer, and it wasn't his overbite. That's why the Mercury mustache orbits to 9 on the 'Stache-o-Meter losing a point for laying a goose egg with Flash . . ."aaah aaah" Gordon. What can we say, "It's a Kind of Mustache."

TOP FIVE ROCKERS WHO RECENTLY ROCKED THE 'STACHE

1. RIVERS CUOMO, WEEZER

2. FRANZ NICOLAY, THE HOLD STEADY

3. CARLOS D., INTERPOL

4. BRANDON FLOWERS, THE KILLERS

5. EUGENE HUTZ, GOGOL BORDELLO

TOP FIVE FRONT MEN WITH FACIAL HAIR

1. FREDDIE MERCURY, QUEEN

2. JAMES HETFIELD, METALLICA

3. LARRY BLACKMON, CAMEO

4. LIONEL RICHIE, THE COMMODORES

5. CARLOS SANTANA, SANTANA

John Oates

No Mustache? "Say It Isn't So"

Simon and Garfunkel. The Righteous Brothers. Cagney and Lacey. Sometimes good things come in pairs, and when it came to pop music, there was no duo better than Hall and Oates. With hits like "Sara Smile," "Rich Girl," "Maneater," and countless others, the soulful twosome regularly climbed the charts and became the most recognized duo in music history, leaving the Captain and Tennille and, to a lesser degree, Kid 'n Play to eat their dust. But let's not focus on the decades of tremendous success that followed Philadelphia's native sons (well, Oates moved there). Let's examine the most underappreciated musician in rock and roll history, and no, we don't mean Andrew Ridgely. (Next book Andrew, we promise.)

While he might not have had the boyish good looks or the silky hair of his taller partner, Oates was, and still is, a singer and songwriter who is, arguably, trapped in a porn star's body. Born in New York City and raised in the Philadelphia suburbs, this once afroed gem first met Hall in the halls of Temple University. After leaving their respective bands, the two decided to team up and make beautiful music together. Following their debut album, *Whole Oates*, the band had hit upon hit and couldn't have been more popular. They played Live Aid and appeared on "We Are the World," and their videos, which either unfortunately pushed Oates into the background or made him stare into the wrong camera, played around the clock on MTV.

While they've broken up in the past and have each put out their own solo albums, the duo are very much together today, continuing to tour and putting out albums. Still, they haven't been able to recapture that 1970s and 1980s magic, however, because Oates decided to shave off his signature 'stache in the 1990s. The hit makers have taken quite a hit since the mustache made its way off Oates's face.

Who doesn't miss those honey bunches of Oates above the singer's lips? With a 'stache bigger than Ron Jeremy's and more pimpin' than Rudy Ray Moore's "Dolemite," Oates's mustache, matched with a vintage Howard Stern white-guy 'fro, were the perfect complement to Hall's shaved face and silky mane. Seeing John Oates without a mustache is like getting hit with a fish by Lew Zealand. It just doesn't make any sense. Speaking of Lew, he never shaved off his mustache. Then again, he was a Muppet.

'Stache-o-Meter Rating

John Oates supposedly wrote the song "She's Gone" after he got stood up by a chick at a party. Maybe Hall and Oates fans can write a song called "It's Gone" about how he betrayed his fan base by cutting off his biggest attribute. If this were the 1980s, Oates would score a solid 10 on the 'Stache-o-Meter, but we can't jump into a DeLorean and turn back the clock, so he gets a 7. The duo's last studio CD was a Christmas album. Maybe Oates can ask Santa for a new mustache this year?

TOP TEN
GRAMMY-WORTHY MUSTACHES

1.   JOHN OATES

2.   JIM CROCE

3.   FRANK ZAPPA

4.   SONNY BONO

5.   JACK WHITE

6.   JIMI HENDRIX

7.   SAMMY DAVIS JR.

8.   KINKY FRIEDMAN

9.   REV. RUN

10.   LUTHER VANDROSS

Roscoe Orman

The *Real* Bert on *Sesame Street*

Roscoe Orman got his career started by acting on stage. The New York native appeared in a variety of plays in the 1960s, including *Julius Caesar*. He guest-starred on many television shows, including *Sanford and Son* and *Kojak* (a possible precursor to where his head was heading). He hit the big screen in 1974 with *Willie Dynamite*, a film in which he played a pimp. But it was pretty clear early on that Orman's talents were meant for kids on the small screen rather than hookers on a street corner.

Orman is perhaps best known by parents and children as Gordon Robinson on *Sesame Street*. He has shared the screen for four decades with the likes of Big Bird, Aloysius "Snuffy" Snuffleupagus, and Guy Smiley, to name a few. But he was actually the second choice to play good neighbor Gordon after the first actor went the way of the dodo. Luckily for us, he has been a part of our lives for years, which means that his mustache is quite possibly the most underappreciated in television history—honorable mention to the guy who played Isaac on *The Love Boat*.

Who knew that there were two "berts" who lived on Sesame Street? One was the pigeon-loving roommate of Ernie, and of course, the other one was Gordon, a guy with a 'stache that will inspire children for generations to come.

'Stache-o-Meter Rating

At first glance, Orman's upper-lip fuzz could be compared to the likes of Mr. Whipple of "Don't Forget the Charmin" TV commercial fame. But just recently, his well-groomed bert can be mentioned in the same breath as Richard Roundtree's *Shaft*-'stache—with slight homage paid to another children's favorite, *Fraggle Rock*'s own Uncle Traveling Matt. For that, Orman receives a 'Stache-o-Meter score of 9.5.

For years, children all over the world have asked, "Can you tell me how to get, how to get to Sesame Street?" But now as adults, we ponder, "How to get, how to get a Sesame 'stache like that!"

TOP FIVE FANTASTIC FICTIONAL MOUSTACHES

1. DR. SEUSS'S THE LORAX

2. INSPECTOR JACQUES CLOUSEAU

3. *POPEYE'S* WIMPY

4. "THE MARLBORO MAN" DAVID MCLEAN

5. *MONOPOLY'S* RICH UNCLE PENNYBAGS

TOP FIVE KID-FRIENDLY 'STACHES

1. ROSCOE ORMAN

2. LUIGI, *SUPER MARIO BROS.*

3. MR. MCFEELY, *MR. ROGERS' NEIGHBORHOOD*

4. DR. IVO ROBOTNIK, *SONIC THE HEDGEHOG*

5. SPORTACUS, *LAZYTOWN*

Walter Payton

Sweetness with a Touch of 'Stache

They called him "Sweetness" throughout the National Football League for his outstanding and graceful accomplishments both on and off the field. As one of the most well-respected athletes of his generation, the nickname is very much deserved. Walter Payton is arguably the greatest player to ever step on a football field, but beyond the hall-of-fame credentials and the decorated running back's big game performances, it's hard not to notice Payton's push broom. It was a highlight reel right under his nose.

It was the Bears who drafted a bearish-berted Payton in 1975, and despite enduring some losing seasons, he was surely one of its brightest stars. Two years into his career, Payton, despite flulike symptoms, rushed for a then-record 275 yards in a single game. Just to put that into perspective, if one of us were to have flulike symptoms, we would not even be rushing 15 feet to the nearest bathroom.

The team's first winning season during Payton's glory days was in 1984; the same season he broke Jim Brown's career rushing record (Yes *Mars Attacks!* fans, *the* Jim Brown). The only thing hotter that year was Michael Jackson setting his hair on fire during a botched Pepsi commercial. A year later, the star running back, along with his record-breaking bristles, starred in both Chicago's backfield and most notably its "Super Bowl Shuffle" music video.

Altogether, Payton was a nine-time Pro Bowl selection (that's nine more than "The Boz" by the way, but who's counting), a two-time Player of the Year winner, and a Super Bowl Champion with the Chicago Bears. He went on to capture many of the league's rushing records, and when it was all said and done he earned himself a spot among the NFL's elite as a proud member of its 1993 Hall-of-Fame class. Of course, his bust on display in the Football Hall of Fame in Canton, Ohio, captures Payton in all his bert glory.

Upon his retirement from the league in 1987, Payton would rewrite the record books, with over 16,000 yards to his credit. With a cheesy headband around his head, and a fuzzy little bear living above his lip, the graceful and respected Payton is a guaranteed touchdown every time. To be blunt on his bert: Payton did more for Leon Spinks's mustache than Leon Spinks did for his mustache.

'Stache-o-Meter Rating

As versatile as his ability on the field, the fleet-footed football star was always a step and a 'stache above the rest of the NFL. Payton's hairy pushpop scores an 8 on the 'Stache-o-Meter (the equivalent of two field goals and a safety). As number 34's legacy and inspirational life continue to affect some of today's most talented stars almost ten years after his untimely death, one thing is for certain: Walter Payton was sweetness with a sweet 'stache.

TOP FIVE FOOTBALL FUZZ WITH SOME KICK

1. NICK LOWERY
2. SCOTT PLAYER
3. EFREN HERRERA
4. SEAN LANDETA
5. RUSSELL ERXLEBEN

Doctor That 'Stache

Whenever Oprah Winfrey throws her weight around, someone becomes a star, and that's not a fat joke. Whether it's lending her support toward then-Senator Barack Obama in 2008 or launching the careers of Dr. Phil McGraw and, to a far lesser degree, her BFF, Gayle King, the talk-show queen has made a career out of making other people's careers.

Dr. Phil, in particular, has benefited most of all thanks to the big "O." Let's face it, before Winfrey put him on her show, the psychologist was helping a precious few. Now, he's a star attraction, instantly going from a rusty Chevy Nova to a polished Rolls Royce.

Whether it's transvestites looking to reconnect with their family or overweight people trying to see their feet again, McGraw has offered advice to anyone who will listen—and even those who won't. After decades of making a career of telling people what they should do, however, it's time the good doctor takes a bit of his own medicine. He needs to talk less and groom his mustache more. Though more on that after this short bio commercial break.

McGraw was born in Oklahoma, raised in North Texas, and went to college on a University of Tulsa football scholarship. When his team got sacked hard (reports say they lost one game 100 to 6—that's worse than a Dick Butkus *My Two Dads* cameo fumble), he set out to become a psychologist like his dad at Midwestern State University. There, he received his bachelor's degree in the field, and earned a master's in experimental psychology a year later. Ever the prize pupil, he earned his Ph.D. in clinical psychology in 1979 from the University of North Texas.

After private practice and conducting seminars, McGraw started his own legal-consulting firm, which Oprah Winfrey employed in the mid-1990s, and that led to regular appearances on her couch; best-selling books; and in 2002, his very own syndicated show. To this day, the series is second only to Ms. Oprah in the daytime ratings, and he's clearly become a pop culture icon in that he had a Muppet doppelganger created for him on *Sesame Street* called Dr. Feel.

While he's found many successes and has helped countless people overcome their problems with his commanding "get real" approach, McGraw's had a few problems of his own. He's had a few legal issues; his line of diet supplements went belly up; and, tragically, in 2006 he appeared in the film *Scary Movie 4*. In addition, his efforts in January 2008 to stage an intervention for Britney Spears, her shaved head, and her family, failed miserably.

But overall, Dr. Phil has been as unstoppable as Ichiro Suzuki on roller skates in the rain. His mustache, as noted, however, could use some counseling. While it's not a complete disaster like the straggly one Orlando Bloom tried out after he wrapped up the last *Pirates of the Caribbean* movie, it's not quite living up to its potential. The salt-and-peppered follicles are merely a step above the fake bert William Hurt sported in *The Incredible Hulk*. To put it bluntly, because that's how Dr. Phil rolls on his show, his mustache is a little rough around the edges.

'Stache-o-Meter Rating

Dr. Phil McGraw has helped so many battle substance abuse, depression, and countless other social issues, but the psychologist needs to "get real" and manage his mustache a little better. In a battle of famous doctors, McGraw places somewhere between "Dr. J" and Dr. Joyce Brothers, and for that, his yearning mid-face yarn gets a 6 on the 'Stache-o-Meter. (On a side note, in a battle of Oprah's main mustachioed men, McGraw easily gets crushed by Winfrey-mainstay Stedman Graham.) We know it means well, but it's time to call a mustache intervention.

TOP FIVE
MUSTACHIOED MODERATORS

1. DR. PHIL MCGRAW

2. JUDGE JOE BROWN

3. MONTEL WILLIAMS

4. GERALDO RIVERA

5. JOHN STOSSEL

TOP TEN INSPIRING
MOVIE MUSTACHES

1. PAUL NEWMAN, *THE STING*

2. EDDIE MURPHY, *48 HOURS*

3. JACKIE GLEASON, *SMOKEY AND THE BANDIT*

4. JAMES BROLIN, *THE CAR*

5. DAVID HYDE PIERCE, *WET HOT AMERICAN SUMMER*

6. ANTHONY HOPKINS, *LEGENDS OF THE FALL*

7. MICHAEL PALIN, *MONTY PYTHON'S LIFE OF BRIAN*

8. ORSON WELLES, *THE STRANGER*

9. ROBERT REDFORD, *BUTCH CASSIDY AND THE SUN-DANCE KID*

10. DAMON WAYANS, *MAJOR PAYNE*

Richard Pryor

A "Bustin' Loose" 'Stache

No one could ever accuse Richard Pryor of pulling a Milli Vanilli. The legendary comedian was a complete original who didn't care who was offended, who laughed, or who ended up in jail or the hospital—even if it was oftentimes himself.

A confrontational but always side-splittingly funny comedian, the man inspired countless others who came before and after him, and drew controversy by dropping more N-bombs than Tupac and Suge at a Death Row Records clam bake. While his risqué humor is the legacy he leaves behind, his mustache was a wonderful polar opposite of the man himself. Thick and juicy like a BK Broiler, Pryor's 'stache was never something to laugh at, and was always lush and neatly groomed.

To say Pryor had a hard upbringing would be like saying Olivia Newton-John only gave a few men erections with her workout music video for "Physical." Born in 1940, Pryor, who rocked a nice afro as well by the way, was raised in a whore house. Born the son of a prostitute and pimp, he was kicked out of school at an early age and ultimately enlisted in the army, where he landed in jail. Eventually, Pryor became a nightclub emcee, and burst onto the New York City comedy circuit.

Although his career started off tame, by the late 1960s, Pryor would reach his stride Lenny Bruce–style, commenting openly on social issues—notably racism—and scoring one hit comedy album after another. In 1974, his unflinching album *That N****r's Crazy* led to larger acclaim while likely making clean-cut Bill Cosby cover his ears like there was no tomorrow.

After writing for television (he wrote for such series as *The Flip Wilson Show* and the Desmond Wilson fuzzfest *Sanford and Son*), Pryor made dozens of films, most of which were bad and starred Gene Wilder. His films included *Stir Crazy*, *The Mack*, and *Lady Sings the Blues*, but it was his initial string of concert films that truly capitalized on the comedian's magic. (On an unrelated note, we're convinced his movie *The Toy* set African Americans back at least one decade, but that's neither here nor there, and while we'll give him props for cowriting the classic *Blazing Saddles*, we still, twenty-five years later, ask ourselves why he was in *Superman III*.)

Off-camera, Pryor was known as difficult, abusive, and self-destructive. In 1980, he set himself on fire after freebasing cocaine and was burned over half of his body. In his later years, he was crippled by multiple sclerosis, and ultimately succumbed to the condition in 2005. However, we'll always remember the lively jolt of energy he was. Ditto for that mustache of his, which looked like a black towel on a rack made of lips. It was as if one took Gene Wilder's curly top, spun it around ever so tightly, and superglued it onto Pryor's face.

'Stache-o-Meter Rating

The best way to describe Richard Pryor's mustache would be with a patented N-word: natural. The 'stache fit effortlessly, appearing as if Paul Winfield's and Keith David's mustaches had simply combusted together. For that, the Pryor push broom scores a solid 9.5 on the 'Stache-o-Meter. If his mustache ever jumped off his face and attended an open mic night, it'd easily win over the crowd with its commanding stage presence.

TOP TEN FUNNY MEN WITH FUNNY MUSTACHES

1. RICHARD PRYOR
2. EDDIE MURPHY
3. GALLAGHER
4. STEVE HARVEY
5. DENNIS WOLFBERG
6. MARTIN LAWRENCE
7. ROBIN HARRIS
8. GROUCHO MARX
9. DAVE CHAPPELLE
10. BERNIE MAC

Burt Reynolds

Put that Mustache in the Smithsonian

Burt Reynolds hasn't exactly made the best career choices. Throughout the years, the legendary actor has reportedly turned down the roles of James Bond, Han Solo, *Die Hard*'s John McClane, and Jack Nicholson's Oscar-winning astronaut in *Terms of Endearment*. While he hasn't used the best judgment when making pivotal acting decisions (we're guessing one filmgoer actually liked *Cop and a Half*—probably Burt buddy Dom DeLuise), the actor has maintained his iconic status in Hollywood for decades for one thing and one thing alone: He has the most recognizable mustache in pop culture history.

Burton Leon Reynolds is a high-class star with the highest class 'stache. For over forty years, Reynolds has appeared in roughly 90 films and 300 television episodes. While he's shaved off his 'stache here or there, the actor always comes back to the calling card that is his mustache. And why shouldn't he?

A Reynolds mustache grown at 75 percent is the average man's mustache's grown at 100 percent. The love child of Yanni and New York Jet Mark Gastineau, the Burt bert always seems fully grown, well-groomed, and worn to perfection. You can search every nook and cranny, but you will always come back to the Reynolds mustache, which has been as reliable as LifeCall (now referred to as Life Alert, the service that helped that old woman after she had fallen and couldn't get up).

But, let's be fair. There's more to Burt than his bert. The Georgia native was a star college football player and was on his way to the pros before an injury stopped him dead in his tracks. Before long, he ditched college and headed to the Big Apple to become an actor. He made appearances on such television shows as *Gunsmoke* and had forgettable roles in forgettable films like *100 Rifles* and *Sam Whiskey*. Reynolds didn't really hit his stride until the 1972 classic *Deliverance*. Taking it in the backwoods as Lewis Medlock led to fame and a string of hits for the star. It also led to a real emergence of that magnificent mustache.

Following the gridiron flick *The Longest Yard*, the actor rocked the 'stache for the hit *Smokey and the Bandit* and its two crappy sequels. Fueled by the those films, *Cannonball Run*, and even *The Best Little Whore House in Texas*, Reynolds owned the box office from the late 1970s to the early 1980s with his handsome looks, star power, charisma, and charm.

But tag-teaming with fellow badass Clint Eastwood in *City Heat*, a film that was ironically not so hot, Reynolds's career began to fade quicker than an Etch-A-Sketch drawing. Luckily, he found success on the small screen during the 1990s with *Evening Shade*, a popular sitcom that won him an Emmy and allowed him to work with the late great character actor Michael Jeter, who had a legendary mustache of his own and chased a mouse years later in *The Green Mile*.

For the past two decades, Reynolds has remained a presence on the big screen, but it's mostly been hit or miss. His turn as a horny southern governor opposite Demi Moore in *Striptease* failed to arouse audiences and critics (perhaps because he went 'stacheless?) but his turn in *Boogie Nights* quickly redeemed him. Portraying a porn director earned him a Golden Globe, an Oscar nomination, and an opportunity to work alongside a post–Funky Bunch Marky Mark.

More success has followed Reynolds, including recent hits like a remake of his own *The Longest Yard*, but for the most part he still doesn't select his roles wisely. Take his emaciated bearded turn as Boss Hogg in the *Dukes of Hazzard* remake from a few years ago.

Offscreen, Reynolds has made his share of headlines, whether it's for womanizing (he's dated everyone from Dinah Shore to Sally Field), posing nude for *Cosmo* (his mustache never looked so good), slapping a camera man a few years back, or that much-publicized divorce from actress Loni Anderson. But throughout it all, the actor has continued to stay relevant in an industry he once ruled over—and that's with or without his 'stache. But like his toupee, we'd prefer he leave it on.

'Stache-o-Meter Rating

He may have shot blanks with *Sharky's Machine*, *Rent-a-Cop*, and *Stick*, but Burt Reynolds fires a bert-o-rific 9.9 on the 'Stache-o-Meter. The legendary actor loses just .1 percent on the sole basis that he finds it necessary to shave his mustache from time to time or sport a beard to disguise the fuzz above. Seeing Reynolds without his mustache is like seeing Dom De Luise without a sandwich: It's not right. That guy gets more miles out of his mustache than Bo Darville got out of his Pontiac Trans-Am Firebird.

TOP TEN TV DADS WITH MUSTACHES

1. ALEX KARRAS, *WEBSTER*

2. JOHN ASTIN, *THE ADDAMS FAMILY*

3. EARLE HYMAN, *THE COSBY SHOW*

4. GERALD MCRANEY, *MAJOR DAD*

5. REGINALD VEL JOHNSON, *FAMILY MATTERS*

6. JOHN ANISTON, *DAYS OF OUR LIVES*

7. TIM REID, *SISTER, SISTER*

8. SHERMAN HEMSLEY, *THE JEFFERSONS*

9. NED FLANDERS, *THE SIMPSONS*

10. BURT REYNOLDS, *EVENING SHADE*

Lionel Richie

Once, Twice, Three Times a Mustache

They say all good things must come to an end. If that statement is indeed true, it explains why the Thompson Twins broke up, why MTV's *Remote Control* went off the air, and most importantly, why Lionel Richie woke up one morning and said, "Hey, I want more hair on my face."

Back in the day, there wasn't a bigger star than Lionel Richie. Equipped with an afro that would make Art Garfunkel weep uncontrollably (even now) and a mustache that would make Paul Simon green with envy (even now), the soulful singer/songwriter melted hearts and shook moneymakers with chart-topper after chart-topper in the 1970s and 1980s.

Richie was born in Alabama, and actually made his mark at first as a pro-caliber tennis player, but music was his true calling. After leading the Commodores in dance hits like "Brick House" and ballads like "Easy," Richie hit it solo in the early '80s and never looked back. His self-titled album was a smash in 1982, and the follow-up a year later *Can't Slow Down* was even bigger.

An unstoppable force with an unstoppable knack for power vocals—and to a lesser degree really bad clothing—Richie scored Grammys for songs like "Truly," became a fixture on MTV with videos like the schmaltzy "Dancing on the Ceiling," and the engaging art school drama "Hello." He even landed an Oscar in 1985 for "Say You, Say Me," the theme song from some crappy Russian tap-dancing movie. We still have absolutely no idea what that song or the movie meant by the way.

Arguably the biggest triumph of the performer's career—aside from perhaps the winning ballad "Ballerina Girl"—was U.S.A. for Africa. In 1985, he cowrote "We Are the World" with Michael Jackson, a song that moved the nation, exposed world hunger, helped raise millions, and most importantly, provided Dan Ackroyd with an appearance in a music video for no apparent reason.

Despite all his accomplishments, Richie turned his back on his fan base and "Penny Lovers" all over the world when he let his facial hair get out of control. Since the early 1990s, Richie has sported either a goatee or a beard and has left the 'stache behind. Apparently love wasn't endless after all.

Pointed ever so slightly down, like a hairy boomerang, Lionel's lush hairy lip cup was the wicked stepson of deer-killing rocker Ted Nugent and *Reno 911*'s nuthug lover Lt. Jim Dangle. To put it bluntly, Richie's mustache was "easy like Sunday morning." Now it's as hard as, say, a Monday mid-afternoon.

'Stache-o-Meter Rating

Seeing Lionel Richie without a neatly trimmed mustache is like seeing the carnival's bearded lady with only a mustache. It's just not meant to be. While there's no mistaking his talent as a singer and songwriter, Richie made a bad career decision when he opted for more shag and less Motown mustache. The old Richie would've gotten a 10 on the 'Stache-o-Meter, but because it's long gone (like his unnecessary "Ceiling" ponytail), he drops two and a half points to a 7.5. Richie's decision to forgo the fuzz was the biggest flop in R&B since Jermaine Jackson dropped his debut solo album.

TOP FIVE
"WE ARE THE WORLD" WHISKERS

1. LIONEL RICHIE
2. JOHN OATES
3. STEVIE WONDER
4. SMOKEY ROBINSON
5. MARLON JACKSON

Geraldo Rivera

Mustache-at-Large

Aside from Theodore Roosevelt and perhaps Jimi Hendrix, no man in history has ever put his mustache as much in harm's way as Geraldo Rivera. Since his career began, the television personality/ journalist has gone to battle by covering wars, exposing the unexposable, and sharing the stage with everyone from cross-dressing priests to Satan worshippers. Through it all, he's collected his fair share of battle scars (a broken nose during a show taping and a sore fanny courtesy of Hurricane Ike), but luckily for us, his mustache has remained intact, and unlike the man himself, it's always been quite uplifting.

Rivera, born in Manhattan to a Puerto Rican father and Jewish mother, started his career as an attorney before landing on New York City's *Eyewitness News* as an investigative reporter and ultimately on a pre–John Stossel *20/20* for nearly a decade. While the 1970s focused on investigative journalism (he broke such stories as Elvis's overdose and the unearthed footage of the Kennedy assassination), the late 1980s and early 1990s saw Rivera turn into a no-holds-barred television personality. In 1987, he ushered in the era of "trash TV" by hosting his own syndicated talk show. While rivals Oprah Winfrey and Phil Donahue focused on domestic issues and celebrity interviews, Rivera put a large spotlight on extreme guests like hermaphrodites looking for love and skinheads looking for hate.

While Rivera's show was a hit across the board, his appeal extended far beyond men in red dresses and white hoods. His various specials, notably the 1986 telecast *The Mystery of Al Capone's Vault*, scored big in the ratings, and a broken nose he sustained during a show entitled "Teen Hate Mongers" became front-page material across all news services. In terms of the former, if only we had that hour back, as Rivera's laborious excavation found nothing buried underneath. Even a rerun of *Remington Steele* or *Falcon Crest* would've been more enjoyable. In fact, the only thing more disappointing that year was when Mrs. Garrett left Tootie and the girls at the Eastland School for the Peace Corps.

The Geraldo Rivera Show ran for eleven years and helped pave the way for future sleaze scholars like Morton Downey Jr. and Jerry Springer. From the mid-1990s to the present, Rivera has gone back to his roots with respectable journalism, launching *Rivera Live* on CNBC in 1994 and following that up with his own show on the FOX News Channel. In his career, Rivera has done it all.

He's covered just about every international crisis (from Bosnia to Afghanistan), and has racked up award after award, including the prestigious George Foster Peabody Award.

While Rivera may flip-flop between "trash TV" host and credible journalist, his mustache has remained the same all the way. Yes, we've buried the lead. Rivera's mustache is like exposing a big story. You just can't wait to talk about it. And while former mustachioed stars like John Oates and Alex Trebek have toyed with our emotions by shaving their infamous 'staches off their famous faces, Rivera realizes the Shangri-La below his nose is pure gold. The man might not have found anything digging up Capone's vault, but we all found a treasure on his face. And, it's not buried. It's there for the world to see.

'Stache-o-Meter Rating

Despite garnering his share of acclaim early on in his career, Rivera has long been criticized for his journalistic ethics, or lack thereof. While that can be debated, his mustache-moral values never can be. For that, his 'stache—groomed to American diplomat John Bolton perfection with a slab of Texas Rangers' flash-in-the-pan Pete Incaviglia for dexterity—scores Rivera a commanding 9 on the 'Stache-o-Meter. If President Reagan was the Teflon president, Rivera has the Teflon mustache. Nobody can touch it. He may be half Puerto Rican and half Jewish, but he's all mustache.

TOP FIVE WHO DELIVERED THE 'STACHE WHEN WE WANTED THE NEWS

1. WALTER CRONKITE

2. RON BURGUNDY

3. PAT O'BRIEN

4. GERALDO RIVERA

5. ROLAND SMITH

Borat Sagdiyev

Mustache . . . Is Nice!

His sister may rank as the number four prostitute in all of Kazakhstan, but when it comes to mustaches, there's no mistaking who places number one on that country's list of facial-hair accomplishments: Borat Sagdiyev.

A respected journalist with an unorthodox interviewing style, this personality has essentially become a walking billboard for "the greatest country in the world." Sagdiyev has gone to great lengths to inform America that Kazakhstan is the place to be. It's the best exporter of potassium, it takes pride in the fact it invented toffee, and above all, it offers the cleanest prostitutes next to Turkmenistan.

Whores aside, ever the investigative reporter, Sagdiyev has tried to expose the atrocities of his country by speaking out against homosexuals, gypsies, and Jews—most notably the notorious "Jew Claw." He also is synonymous with high fives, and never fails to mention that he enjoys sex preferably with someone with a "shaved vazhïn."

Throughout his career, the Kazakh journalist has covered such epic stories as "The Running of the Jews," has interviewed such dignitaries as Alan Keyes, and even sang his homeland's national anthem to a capacity American crowd. The latter was seen in his 2006 movie-film entitled *Borat: Cultural Learnings of America for Make Benefit Glorious Nation of Kazakhstan.*

The movie chronicled his trip across America, which was fueled by a desire to meet his crush, former *Baywatch* babe Pamela Anderson, and included a naked hotel fight with his producer Azamat Bagatov. The latter proved that the Kazakh native has taken more balls to the chin than Johnny Bench. Above all, the film made Sagdiyev an international star, leading to appearances on *Saturday Night Live* and *Live with Regis and Kelly.*

Numerous television appearances and ball shots aside, there's no question the most appealing thing about Sagdiyev, next to perhaps his trademark gray suit with high-powered shoulder pads, is the man's amazing upper-lip whiskers that best bear a resemblance to John Oates's push broom from the 1982 music video of "I Can't Go for That (No Can Do)" matched with an extended form of Anna Nicole Smith's crying judge Lawrence Korda sans the peach cobbler fuzz.

The journalist's mustache hangs like the sleeve of a wizard's robe, covering his entire nose-to-mouth region and even extending ever so neatly to his cheeks. To get right to it, his mustache makes you want to scream "*Wawaweewa,*" and then, um, dry hump something.

'Stache-o-Meter Rating

Borat Sagdiyev has been accused of being a sexist, a homophobe, and an anti-Semite. That may be true, but the one clear thing the man is guilty of is having a mustache that was born to be in pictures. It'll be hard to find one watchdog group who wouldn't agree that his mustache is distinguished, respectable, and universally acceptable. For that, Sagdiyev scores a "very nice" 9 on the 'Stache-o-Meter. To sum up, Borat's bert should soon surpass potassium as Kazakhstan's biggest export. As for prostitution? Not so much. Dziekuje.

TOP TEN
KOSHER 'STACHES

1. RON JEREMY
2. GROUCHO MARX
3. LOU JACOBI
4. SACHA BARON COHEN
5. GABE KAPLAN
6. JERRY STILLER
7. BOB DYLAN
8. ALFRED STIEGLITZ
9. ALBERT EINSTEIN
10. SAMMY DAVIS JR.

The Poor Man's Burt Reynolds?

Thomas "Tom" Selleck's first television appearance was as a guest on *The Dating Game* in 1967, when he was a college senior. Despite his good looks and charm, he did not achieve the height of his fame until some fifteen years later. After appearances on such shows as *The Young and the Restless* and *Marcus Welby, MD*, Selleck finally made it big playing the title role of ex-Navy Seal and Vietnam Vet Thomas Sullivan Magnum IV on *Magnum P.I.* His decision to don a Detroit Tigers cap, a Hawaiian shirt, and a bert that wouldn't quit personified the actor's career. His good fortune took a hit when his role in Magnum kept him from accepting the lead role of Indiana Jones in Steven Spielberg's *Raiders of the Lost Ark*.

Even so, he became a television star. He was everyone's favorite private dick, gaining a legion of female fans who marveled at his body and budding chest hair—and of course, his sexy 'stache. Before long, the Detroit native established himself as one of the hottest stars with facial hair on the 1980s small screen—second only to Michael Gross's beard on *Family Ties*.

After a successful run of eight years, Selleck left behind his *Magnum* binoculars, but he carried his bert with him to the big screen. In 1987 he landed the coveted role of Peter Mitchell, one of three bachelors forced into parenthood in the classic romp *Three Men and a Baby*, opposite fellow 1980s immortals Ted Danson and Steve Guttenberg. Throughout the rest of the decade and the 1990s, it was win some/lose some for Selleck. He appeared in such lackluster films as *Her Alibi*, *Quigley Down Under*, the 1990 follow-up *Three Men and a Little Lady*, and 1992's *Christopher Columbus: The Discovery*. Selleck returned to top form in the mid- to late '90s, earning critical and public praise for guest appearances as Courteney Cox's love interest on the "Must-See-TV" hit *Friends*. In 1997, he put his career on the line by shaving off his trademark 'stache (and, to a lesser degree, playing a homosexual newsman) in *In & Out*. The 2000s have seen Selleck thrive on and off the small screen—thankfully with his bert fully intact.

'Stache-o-Meter Rating

You might question some of his choices in film or television, but there's no mistaking the appeal of Selleck's mustache. His bert gives an Oscar- and Emmy Award–winning performance whenever it's on his face. It has stood the test of time, combining a little Tom Skerritt and Chef Boyardee (sans the gray)—with a little Meathead from *All in the Family* thrown in for good measure.

Give or take an outburst from Rosie O'Donnell about the NRA or a shaved upper lip, Selleck has enjoyed a much-deserved, prosperous career. As a matter of fact, for a man in his sixties, he's still got many women willing to go on a mustache ride. And for that, he ranks a solid 9 on the 'Stache-o-Meter.

TOP FIVE MUSTACHES MORE FAMOUS THAN THE MEN THEMSELVES

1. LARRY BLACKMON, CAMEO

2. J. T. TAYLOR, KOOL AND THE GANG

3. MR. POTATO HEAD

4. SINBAD

5. SAL FASANO, BASEBALL PLAYER

We Preferred Siskel, But This Gene Will Do

Many films are flawed, but when it comes to reviewers, celebrated *Today Show* film critic Gene Shalit consistently turns up a reliable winner.

Yes, Siskel and Ebert may have had their thumbs up and thumbs down, the *New York Times*'s Pauline Kael may have had her routine ruthless wit, and *In Living Color*'s Blaine and Antoine might have had their "two snaps with a twist and a kiss," but Shalit had signature quips, an array of colorful puns, and even more colorful big cheesy bowties. But make no mistake about it: This longtime personality made his mark with that big old bushy handlebar mustache that complemented his Art Garfunkel–inspired white afro. His 'stache could easily rate four stars from the shrewdest of critics.

Throughout thirty-plus years, Shalit has been a mainstay on that NBC morning show, although he's rumored to have not gotten along well with former cohost Bryant Gumbel, and drew criticism from GLAAD a few years back for his review of *Brokeback Mountain*. No word on whether he was jealous of Willard Scott, who helped old people celebrate milestone birthdays.

In addition Shalit had an extensive career as a writer, penning books and contributing stories for various publications, including *TV Guide* and *Seventeen*. He's also appeared as himself in a variety of television shows and films, and even popped up to steal scenes away from Joe Piscopo in the legendary 1986 "Let's Go Mets" video.

But again, there's more to Shalit than a quippy line or two or dozen. His mustache, much like his review of *The Illusionist* last year, "casts a magical spell." A sequel to Leroy Neiman's mustache but slightly better in that it's as if it vomited down the sides of his mouth a little more and has been sprinkled with a touch of Father Guido Sarducci, the mustache sticks out on a face that is already vibrant. Funny glasses, thick eyebrows, and a silly hairdo aside, if Shalit's 'stache were an actor, it'd be a shoo-in to win a Best Supporting Actor honor.

'Stache-o-Meter Rating

With his Mr. Potato Head looks and signature style and wit, Shalit is arguably the most recognizable film critic in history. Similarly, his mustache rates as one of the most recognizable as well. It's always been hair today, and never gone tomorrow, as Gene might say, and that's why we give Shalit's overgrown facial hair a solid 9 on the 'Stache-o-Meter.

Hate the Sheik; Don't Hate the 'Stache

In a fantasy world filled with dastardly villains and evil wrongdoers such as Gargamel, Darth Vader, and Cobra Kai Sensei John Kreese, it's hard not to mention Hossein Khosrow Ali Vaziri in the same breath. Of course, the latter mentioned badass is better known by his wrestling moniker: the Iron Sheik.

In 1979, a few years after an assistant coaching stint for the U.S. Olympic team, the amateur wrestling star and former bodyguard for the Shah of Iran made the transformation into a heel by shaving his head bald, curling the toes of his wrestling boots, and growing out the now signature Sheik 'stache.

Wrestling as the Great Hossein Arab for a brief time, it wasn't until 1983 that he made a name for himself by entering the WWE as the dreaded and hated Iron Sheik. The Sheik gave Americans the worst holiday gift ever that year when he ended Bob Backlund's six-year reign as World Champion the day after Christmas. The mustachioed madman from Iran was awarded the coveted title when "The Pride of White Plains," Arnold Skaaland, threw in the towel while Backlund was locked in the Sheik's Camel Clutch.

During his month-long reign of terror, the Sheik played on the real-life hatred Americans had toward Iran at the time (the epitome of a "cheap pop" by the way) and defeated "the best of the best," which included the likes of a pre–Samba-Simba Tony Atlas and per-renial mid-carder Tito Santana. After dropping the belt to the Hulk-ster, the Sheik started a bitter rivalry with another hugely popular whiskered wrestler and G.I. Joe figure known as Sgt. Slaughter. While the green-tongued animal, George Steele, was busy chowing down on turnbuckles, these two grizzled grapplers were beating each other bloody in their now legendary "boot camp rules" matches.

Sporting the most menacing facial accessories in the ring since Ox Baker's black bushy bristles, the Iron Sheik reached the top of the mountain again when he captured the WWE Tag Team Championship with his partner and part-time musical treasure, Nikolai Volkoff. For roughly two years, both foreign-born stars kept a steady strangle-hold on every tag team in the federation while being managed by both "Classy" Freddie Blassie and "The Doctor of Style" Slick.

It wasn't until 1987 that the Sheik's career, not to mention the realness of pro wrestling, were called into question. One day Teh-ran's own Iron Sheik and supposed American adversary "Hacksaw" Jim Duggan were pulled over together on the Jersey Turnpike as cohorts in some illegal extracurricular activities. The legitamacy of the feud was tainted, and eventually Sheik's days as a WWE villain were over.

Sheik would spend the rest of the 1980s and early 1990s around in several other wrestling circles. He finally got the call by WWE in 1991 to appear alongside his former enemy Sgt. Slaughter as an Iraqi sympathizer. Although he was now being billed as Col. Mustafa, the Sheik's loyal fans (all two of them) were delighted to see that his custom-made mustache was still intact.

While Sheik-a-mania never caught on, everyone could agree that the wrestler's mustache—a lifelike version of Wonder Woman villain Egg Fu's—was a classic. He may have caught instant heat for spitting on America in his incomprehensible promos, but one thing everyone could agree on was that the Sheik's 'stache was chic.

'Stache-o-Meter Rating

As one of wrestling's most unforgettable characters, the Iron Sheik continues to go head-to-head with Father Time. Just recently he was inducted into the WWE Hall of Fame, was victorious in the first and only Wrestle-Mania Gimmick Battle Royal, and has become a fan favorite guest on *The Howard Stern Show*. Despite a controversial career that has had its share of ups and downs (heavy on the downs), the always outspoken, often anti-American Sheik has been pro-mustache all the way. For that, we give him a side-suplexing 8.5 on the 'Stache-o-Meter. Hulk Hogan may have won the battle, but the Iron Sheik won the mustache war.

Morgan Spurlock

Super-sized 'Stache

Documentary filmmaker Morgan Spurlock made waves in 2004 with the release of *Super Size Me*, a film in which he chronicled his decision to eat nothing but McDonald's for each meal, each day, for thirty days. While his startling actions and subsequent poor health at the hands of the Grimace company made him a star, a bigger risk he took was trying to be taken seriously while sporting one alarming Fu Manchu.

Not since the days of baseball great Luis Tiant and metal god James Hetfield has a man so boldly tried to gain stardom by rocking a hairy magnet on his face. Spurlock has done a lot more than simply be the worst thing to happen to McDonald's since the creation of the McLean Deluxe.

Like NBA legend Jerry West and Olympic Red Bull Mary Lou Retton, Spurlock was born and raised in West Virginia. Deep down, though, he's a New Yorker. He graduated from New York University and, for the most part, has resided in the Big Apple ever since. While he eventually would start spreading the news on the fat contents of a fast-food chain, Spurlock initially made his mark in Manhattan by becoming a respectable playwright and web sensation. *I Bet You Will*, which had ordinary people doing crazy things (who wants a glass of mayo?), took off on the Internet and eventually television, but he wouldn't reach his peak until those tasty McNuggets came calling.

In 2003, Spurlock got the idea for *Super Size Me* after seeing a report about two girls suing the chain for leading them to be overly chubby. From there, he started the all-McDonald's diet, and as documented in the film, gained twenty-five pounds and suffered liver damage.

The movie put McDonald's under a microscope, earned the filmmaker an Oscar nomination and acclaim, and led to a similar-themed hit cable series called *30 Days*. That show chronicles himself and/or others living a month of someone else's life. (We personally would give anything to become *Night Court*'s Richard Moll for a month, but only if it was when he was actually on that popular series.)

In 2008, Spurlock's second film *Where in the World Is Osama Bin Laden?* was released, but his attempt and failure to track down the skinny terrorist with that frizzy beard failed to catch as much buzz as his first film. As far as we're concerned, Spurlock could try to track down Carmen Sandiego or even that annoying a cappella group who composed the catchy theme song, and we'd still be captivated because of his inquisitive mustache.

Whenever Spurlock is on screen, which is fairly often but never as excessively as fellow documentarian Michael Moore in his movies, we're instantly sucked in by a mustache that looks like *The Great Spacecoaster*'s Gary Gnu hairline placed solely on the sides of his mouth. Making the mustache style okay for men who aren't Chinese villains, Spurlock's Filet-o-Fuzz is even more appetizing than a Big Mac with large fries.

'Stache-o-Meter Rating

Morgan Spurlock's middle name is Valentine. This comes as no surprise. What's not to love about the man's filmmaking style and mouth-watering 'stache? Earning a quarter-pounding 8 on the 'Stache-o-Meter, Spurlock proves that in a world of apple pies and Happy Meals, he'll always be Mayor McMustache.

TOP FIVE OSCAR-WINNING MUSTACHES

1. DANIEL DAY-LEWIS, *THERE WILL BE BLOOD*

2. BEN KINGSLEY, *GANDHI*

3. DAVID NIVEN, *SEPARATE TABLES*

4. ART CARNEY, *HARRY AND TONTO*

5. MARLON BRANDO, *THE GODFATHER*

Commander in 'Stache

Throughout U.S. history, presidents have had their share of loving pets. Richard Nixon had Checkers, Bill Clinton had Buddy, and William Howard Taft . . . well, he had a furry little creature his nose walked every morning, afternoon, and evening.

The last president to sport facial hair, Taft made his nose tresses an authoritative piece of U.S. history as a commanding presence on the commander in chief's face.

Born in 1857, Taft graduated from Yale and became a respected lawyer in Cincinnati. He eventually became a federal judge, and that notoriety led to presidential missions and appointments, including secretary of war under President Theodore Roosevelt. The fellow-mustached Rough Rider was so fond of Taft's work, he nominated him as his successor in the Oval Office.

Much to progressives' and conservatives' delight, Taft defeated William Jennings Bryan to become the twenty-seventh president of the United States. While he's credited for his efforts in bettering the postal system and promoting world peace, among other things, Taft's presidency was criticized. Even so, Republicans ended up nominating him for another term in office in 1912. Roosevelt ultimately left the party altogether in favor of the Progressive line and ran against him. Woodrow Wilson ended up defeating the one-two-mustache punch for the presidency, with Taft coming in third.

Taft's biggest successes arguably occurred after he left the White House. He became professor of law at Yale, and in an unprecedented move in U.S. history, and unrepeated still to this day, he was named chief justice of the United States Supreme Court.

Taft's actions and accomplishments as president can be debated, but the sheer brilliance of his mustache never can be denied. The man may have gotten all the headlines for his hefty frame and controversial decisions, but his 'stache is what stood out above all else. This unapologetic yet diplomatic thick and coiled 'stache was a thoroughbred among Oval Office facial hair *Seabiscuit* wanna-bes.

Taft's mustache was truly original (those twirly ends no doubt inspired Rip Taylor and perhaps even Nintendo's Wario). Predecessors like Chester Arthur and Grover Cleveland merely posed flashier versions of, respectively, Civil War general Ambrose Burnside's legendary face coat and the mediocre bushy 'stache that *Saturday Night Live*'s Dan Ackroyd would perfect about 100 years later in his fake ad for the Bassomatic.

'Stache-o-Meter Rating

There's no question William H. Taft's mustache inspired a nation. It was like seeing Rich Uncle Pennybags jump off the Monopoly board and take shape on some pudgy guy's face. For that and so many more reasons, he scores a very presidential 9 on the 'Stache-o-Meter. While he wasn't a clear winner in the White House, we're convinced if the Taft 'stache ever entered the Westminster Kennel Club's competition, it'd be the front-runner for "Best in Show."

TOP FIVE
IN-YOUR-FACE MUSTACHES

1. RIO BLAST, *HE-MAN AND THE MASTERS OF THE UNIVERSE*

2. ROBERT CONRAD, *JAKE AND THE FATMAN*

3. PAUL TEUTUL, *AMERICAN CHOPPER*

4. JAMIE HYNEMAN, *MYTHBUSTERS*

5. ALLAN CORDUNER, *TOPSY-TURVY*

Alex Trebek

We'll Take, "Grow the Mustache Back" for $500, Alex

Forget Anne Murray, Bryan Adams, and even the legendary Rick Moranis. If you ask us, the best thing to come out of Canada has always been one George Alexander "Alex" Trebek.

Canada's native son started his career as a newscaster, but gained acclaim in 1984 by showcasing the sharpest minds in the world as the host of *Jeopardy!* Unfortunately, the Emmy Award–winning host-with-the-most lost something on his climb to the top: that buzz-worthy, Trebekian trim.

For whatever reason, Trebek shaved off his signature 'stache in the 1990s. The decision seemed to be a Sweeps Week ploy to get ratings—no doubt it worked. But it's been ten years, Alex; don't you think it's time to add some "Potpourri" to your face again? Seeing Trebek without a mustache is like spotting Land of Lakes butter on supermarket shelves without that sexy Native American woman on the box.

Forget those zingers he works so hard on, and those vintage eyeglasses aimed to make him look sharper; it's time for the 'stache to make a comeback. Even Will Ferrell, in his spot-on impersonation of Trebek on *Saturday Night Live*, did it with a mustache!

'Stache-o-Meter Rating

Trebek became a U.S. citizen after many years in this country, but the Americanized Alex became just another Chuck Woolery. By conforming to other game show hosts' standards, this card-carrying member of both the Canadian and Hollywood Walks of Fame proved that in a game with its share of losers, a man with a mustache is always a winner.

And for that—with a mustache that resembled Buddy Ebsen's million-dollar one on *The Beverly Hillbillies* with a splice of Burt Lancaster's hairy-lipped portrayal of Moonlight Graham in *Field of Dreams*—retro Trebek enters "Final Jeopardy" with a score of 9 on the 'Stache-o-Meter. And Alex, if you grow it, they will come.

Juan Valdez

A Fictional Character with a Very Real Mustache

The best part of waking up was certainly never Folgers in your cup nor was it buying a $5 latte at Starbucks. It was the crisp and refreshing mug of Colombian coffee courtesy of Juan Valdez that started your day off with a bang. The admirable farmer has always taken care of his customers, has never lowered his standards (even as his own fame and myth grew), and, on occasion, made a few house calls—well in a commercial or two anyway.

While the character has been portrayed by several different actors in various commercials, films, and public appearances throughout the years, his mission and thankfully his mustache have remained the same. Focusing on the former, which for historical purposes is far more important but for this book is far less crucial, Valdez became an iconic figure loved and adored in Colombia. From his first appearance in ads for the National Federation of Coffee Growers of Colombia back in the late 1950s to the introduction of his likeness in a logo in the 1980s to present-day appearances, Valdez has always supported the rights of the country's coffee farmers, and ensures beans that are handpicked and always 100 percent Colombian. But, Valdez's value goes beyond the brew.

He's always had an infectious personality, and yes, a legendary mustache that splendidly protrudes from his face like foam on a latte. Much like a biscotti complements an espresso, Valdez's mustache is the perfect addition to a getup that already includes a trademark straw hat and, for some reason, a mule named Conchetta.

Valdez's bert is as refreshing as any cup of coffee he concocts, and while it pales in comparison to, say, the Village People's Glenn Hughes, it's full-bodied and well defined, with a smooth and consistent feel all around. To put it simply, his java-colored above-the-mouth wallpaper is a slimmed-down version of Ned Flanders 'stache on *The Simpsons* with a splash of fellow Colombian Pablo Escobar's killer mustache thrown in for good measure.

'Stache-o-Meter Rating

7.5

The Starbucks "Siren" is sexier, but Valdez's appeal has had more legs. Why pay an arm and a leg for a cup of coffee at the evil empire when you can get a whole jar with Juan's seal of approval for the same price in your very own home? And, that's just the coffee. What about that 'stache? In a battle of insignia mustaches, Valdez easily defeats the Pringles guy with his foamy mustache, and for that alone, he scores a strong 7.5 on the 'Stache-o-Meter, losing points solely because tea competitor Thomas Lipton's walrus 'stache blows his under the table.

TOP FIVE WHO
SOLD THE 'STACHE

1. SIR THOMAS JOHNSTONE LIPTON
2. JUAN VALDEZ
3. CAP'N CRUNCH
4. HENRY J. HEINZ
5. CHARMIN'S MR. WHIPPLE

Carl Weathers

The 'Stache of Monte Fisto

Carl Weathers, much like Alex Karras, retired from the National Football League and followed his true calling in life: acting. But unlike Karras, whose career path led him to the thankless role of Webster's dad, Weathers became an instant legend with his role as the Muhammed Ali–inspired boxing great Apollo Creed in the *Rocky* films. Aside from his knockout performances in the original classic and three sequels, Weathers has made his mark on American cinema for roughly three decades.

Whether it was his humble beginnings playing Hambone in the blaxploitation classic *Bucktown*, his inspiring performance as a one-handed golf coach in Adam Sandler's *Happy Gilmore* ("it's all in the hips") or his dramatic untimely death in Arnold Schwarzenegger's *Predator*, the actor has regularly stolen scenes from some of Hollywood's heaviest hitters, and has done so effortlessly. Case in point: He took down *Coach*'s Craig T. Nelson in the instant classic *Action Jackson*.

Having said that, Weathers's career will arguably be defined by Creed allowing Rocky Balboa to live out his American dream. Who could forget the epic battles in the first two films, and how he jogged side by side with Balboa in *Rocky III* or how he interacted with Paulie's robot and ultimately threw in the towel for good against a stud of a communist in the fourth installment of the franchise.

But, Dolph Lundgren movies aside, if you ask us, Weathers is the best-known American champion to sport a mustache since Mark Spitz won the gold in Munich. With a mustache that has the subtlety of boxer Ken Norton's pugilistic whiskers but glorified highlights of an old-school Denzel Washington on *St. Elsewhere*, he showed more balls than a happy hour at the Blue Oyster Bar. While we can't confirm rumors that his 'stache helped take down the Cold War in *Rocky IV*, we can clearly say without question that it rivaled James Brown's "Living in America" theatrics in that film. Sylvester Stallone may have had the "Eye of the Tiger," but Weathers had the mustache of a lion.

'Stache-o-Meter Rating

From taking boxing tips from Duke in the *Rocky* films (that guy had a mustache) to his more recent appearances offering acting tips to "never nude" and fellow mustached hero Dr. Tobias Fünke on *Arrested Development*, Carl Weathers is a bona fide actor with a bona fide bert. He may not have had the Mohawk like Mr. T., but Weathers's mustache packs a punch, and for that he Clubber Lang's his way to an even 6 on the 'Stache-o-Meter. Who needs Street Justice when your mustache has street cred?

TOP TEN UNDERAPPRECIATED MOVIE MUSTACHES

1. SEAN CONNERY, *ZARDOZ*

2. TITUS WELLIVER, *GONE BABY GONE*

3. JOHN CANDY, *PLANES, TRAINS AND AUTOMOBILES*

4. EFREN RAMIREZ, *NAPOLEON DYNAMITE*

5. DANIEL DAY-LEWIS, *GANGS OF NEW YORK*

6. BILLY CRUDUP, *ALMOST FAMOUS*

7. JASON SCHWARTZMAN, *THE DARJEELING LIMITED*

8. BILLY BURKE, *TWILIGHT*

9. TIMOTHY DALTON, *THE BEAUTICIAN AND THE BEAST*

10. GARY OLDMAN, *THE DARK KNIGHT*

The Mustache . . . It Works Every Time

Billy Dee Williams's first big break in Hollywood came in the made-for-television tearjerker *Brian's Song*, in which he played Football-Hall-of-Famer Gale Sayers. Like his role in that telefilm, his mustache has, for decades, scored touchdowns and made us fill up with tears—only this time with joy.

Williams always seemed to have star power even before he was a bona fide star. Aside from the aforementioned *Song*, the actor appeared opposite Diana Ross in two highly regarded films, *Mahogany* and *Lady Sings the Blues*, but it wasn't until he was cast in George

Lucas's follow-up to *Star Wars* that his career was launched into hyperspace.

With his *Millenium Falcon*–sized mustache, Williams made his mark in both *The Empire Strikes Back* and *Return of the Jedi* as shady gambler Lando Calrissian. With enough hair under his nose to make even a Wookiee jealous, Williams's character caused Han Solo to be frozen in carbonite, but ultimately he redeemed himself in *Jedi*, helping Chewbacca and his pals take down Boba Fett.

Making the transition from Dagobah to Gotham was easy for Billy Dee. In 1989, he appeared in *Batman* as District Attorney Harvey Dent. The movie, known more for the only appearance of evil henchman Bob the Goon and an awful Prince soundtrack, was a huge box office success and a nice supporting turn for the actor. Appearing in Tim Burton's *Batman* made Williams's whiskers the most prominent mustache in Caped Crusader history since Cesar Romero's Joker in the 1960s television series.

With a successful movie career under his utility belt, Williams's transition to the tube was also seamless. Throughout the years, he's guest-starred on classics like *227* and the short-lived *Gideon's Crossing*, the latter of which starred Burt Reynolds.

Oh, and let's not forget that Williams has got a way with the ladies. He's arguably best known for his suave advertisements for the low-budget malt liquor Colt 45. Who can forget Williams's stylin' and profilin' for the camera and pimpin' a forty-five-ounce bottle of booze with a bunch of hos around him? "Nothing is smoother than an ice-cold bottle of Colt 45" and nothing is smoother than Billy Dee Williams and his brown baggin' bert.

'Stache-o-Meter Rating

Williams, who reportedly has an Ewok living above his upper lip, has been appearing on camera for well over forty years. His mustache, which earns him a 7.5 on the 'Stache-o-Meter, is part Jesse "The Body" Ventura and part Dennis "Oil Can" Boyd. Let us assume that "A long time ago in a galaxy far, far away . . ." Luke had the force but Lando had the fuzz.

TOP FIVE STAR WARS 'STACHES WITH FACIAL FORCE

1. LANDO CALRISSIAN,

   STAR WARS EPISODE VI: THE EMPIRE STRIKES BACK

2. SIR ALEC "OBI WAN" GUINNESS,

   BRIDGE OVER THE RIVER KWAI

3. EWAN "OBI WAN" MCGREGOR,

   MRS. POTTER

4. BIGGS DARKLIGHTER, *STAR WARS EPISODE IV: A NEW HOPE*

5. BREN DERLIN, *STAR WARS EPISODE VI: THE EMPIRE STRIKES BACK*

"Weird Al" Yankovic

Fake Songs, Very Real Mustache

Throughout the years, "Weird Al" Yankovic's song parodies have been mostly hit or miss. For every hilarious send-up like "Smells Like Nirvana," "My Bologna," or "Eat It," there are a slew of uninspired duds like "Yabba-Dabba-Do Now" or "Living with a Hernia" waiting in the wings. Thankfully, the master of parody's mustache back in the day was always reliable, spot-on, and just about the only thing that's 100 percent authentic.

With an upside down V-shaped mustache that combined the power of a *Gone with the Wind* Clark Gable with the fuzzy fortitude of magician Doug Henning's 'stache, the latter of which attempted to cover an overbite that even Freddie Mercury's 'stache couldn't conceal, Yankovic's mustache was delightfully thick and likely itchy and complemented his obscenely large specs and Raggedy Andy perm.

Yankovic's eccentric looks likely played into his fame and fortune, but there's no mistaking the performer's talent and drive. The California native was the valedictorian of his class at the tender age of sixteen and was launched right into a career by sending tapes he made at home to his favorite disc jockey, Dr. Demento. Airplay on that DJ's program led to a string of hit singles and, ultimately, a deal with a major label in the early 1980s. More hits came along, and thanks to the evolution of MTV, Yankovic became a fixture there. Who could forget those memorable "Al TV" specials, which saw the satirist playing all the videos he wanted and putting the spotlight on Harvey the Wonder Hamster?

Since the days of J. J. Jackson and Alan Hunter, Yankovic has enjoyed a long-lasting and fulfilling career, making fun of the songs of everyone from Michael Jackson to Eminem. He's also enjoyed playing polkas with his accordion, an instrument we believe only one of these coauthors' mothers still plays willingly, and he even includes original ditties on each album, but who cares. He's also expanded his repertoire to include films, but his most notable one, *UHF*, which focused on a TV newsroom and featured a prepostal Michael Richards, was torture for the eyes. His mustache, on the other hand, always made for some nice eye candy.

'Stache-o-Meter Rating

In the 1990s, "Weird Al" Yankovic became a changed man. He gave up meat, he shed his trademark glasses (courtesy of LASIK eye surgery), lost his outlandish collection of used-car-salesman Hawaiian shirts, and shaved off those legendary weird whiskers. Ever since, he's not the same funny man, and for that, Al lands a sub-par 7.5 on the 'Stache-o-Meter, a notch below Snoopy's cousin Spike but a step above Jack Black's Nacho Libre. "Weird Al" without a mustache is like bread without butter: It just doesn't taste right.

TOP FIVE FAVORITE MUSTACHES PRAISED ON THECHEAPPOP.COM

1. BETTY WHITE

2. RANCE MULLINIKS

3. ERNIE HUDSON

4. GALLAGHER

5. BERNIE, *WEEKEND AT BERNIE'S*

Yanni

My Big Fat Greek Mustache

Kenny G. did it with a bizarre Sideshow Bob haircut and saxophone. Yo-Yo Ma did it with a bizarre name and a cello. Itzhak Perlman did it with a Wolfgang hairdo and a violin. These varied musicians have achieved unparalleled success and have been so instrumental in instrumental music, but arguably not at the same level of greatness as Yanni has achieved. Doing it with a piano and an undeniable musical mustache (the piano's eighty-ninth key as far as we're considered), the man born Yiannis Hrysomallis has influenced many by simply touching the ivories.

A self-taught musician, Yanni has composed over thirty-five platinum and gold records during his illustrious career. Since the early '90s when Color Me Badd was relevant, grunge was cool, and we still thought wrestling was real, Yanni began his international quest of musical world domination and, with sincere apologies to the late Wesley Willis, he succeeded.

Known best for his awe-inspiring live concert albums, and to a lesser degree for his real-life affair with *Dynasty* and Rock Hudson blonde bombshell Linda Evans, Yanni's sounds have been an integral part of Olympic coverage since around the same time Michael Phelps put on his first pair of swimmies and ventured into the kiddie pool for his first buddy check.

As his music is often described as New Age, Yanni's Grammy-nominated nose fuzz knows no genre. In fact, his chart-topping 'stache is just as touted and recognized as his sold-out concerts across the globe and big hit albums such as *In Celebration of Life*, *Dare to Dream*, and *Runaway Horses* (okay, so the last one is a Belinda Carlisle solo project; we said we were mustache experts, not music people).

With a symphony coming from his nostrils, his first live concert alone, *Yanni Live at the Acropolis*, has sold 7 million more copies worldwide than Buckwheat's cult parody "Wookin' Pa Nub." Who can argue that Yanni's hairy spectacular is more powerful and appealing than the aforementioned Kenny G. mop top?

The former University of Minnesota grad and one-time band member with John Tesh has reached success that few others have achieved. More phenomenal than a blind-folded Dee Brown slam dunk, Yanni's music and mustache collaboration can never be denied.

'Stache-o-Meter Rating

Yanni's upper lip masterpiece is a mustache medley that blends the very best bristles of prop comic and fellow one-named wonder Gallagher with NBA head coach Mike D'Antoni. For this, Yanni earns a chart-topping 8.5 on the 'Stache-o-Meter. Unfortunately, he loses a point for losing not only his 'stache but also his mind in 2006 after a run-in with the law. However, charges were later dropped, and Yanni is planning a return to the global stage. We're sure the music won't miss a beat, but we prefer our Yanni with his legendary lower nose brunette any day of the week.

TOP FIVE MUSICALLY INCLINED MUSTACHES

1. CAB CALLOWAY

2. KEVIN EUBANKS

3. RICHIE "LA BAMBA" ROSENBERG

4. DUKE ELLINGTON

5. IGOR STRAVINSKY

Epilogue

From left to right: Jon Chattman, John Oates, and Rich Tarantino

Final Mustache Musings and a Very Special Thanks to . . .

Sweet 'Stache has been a labor of love for about three years. It's funny
how a book about celebrity mustaches could actually result in so
many sleepless nights and stressful days. But in the end, it was all
worth it and I could never have gotten here without the help of
my close friend and writing partner Rich Tarantino, who not only
offered up zany mustache insights but, more importantly, served
as my Hogan protein shake—keeping me positive and pumped
up during the entire publishing process. I'd like to thank my wife
(my life) for all of her support and understanding, and for dealing

with all those late self-adhesive mustache nights and real mustache days. I'd like to thank my parents for being my cheerleaders, and my friends for supporting my various endeavors (with and sans-'stache) and this book—the latter of which, like it's going out of style. But mustaches, as we all know, will never go out of style. I'd lastly like to thank Brendan O'Neill at Adams Media for believing in that latter statement and the project long before it made its way to his hands.

—Jon Chattman

I would like to thank my tag team partner and close friend Jon Chattman, because a wise man once told me that without a nose there is no mustache, to which I say without Jon there is no *Sweet 'Stache*. Thanks little dude for allowing me to be the Burt Ward to your Adam West. I would like to thank the love of my life, Erica, for all her support and patience during the making of this book. I'd like to thank my mom for always being my biggest fan and my dad—you're still my hero even though you traumatized me when I was five by shaving off your mustache. I'd also like to thank my sister Angela, my brother Allie, my family, my friends, and anyone who aspires to grow a mustache one day because of this book.

—Rich Tarantino

The authors wish to especially thank Adams Media for believing in this project and being upstanding, responsible, and professional publishers throughout the entire process. It's something we value immensely considering past hairy situations with the 'stache. To Brett Underhill for being so insanely talented and smart and for turning out such dynamic caricatures and their mustaches. We'll think of you first if we ever do a pork-chop sideburn book.

To John Oates, thanks for believing and actually "getting" the project, and lending a spectacular foreword that rivals your spectacular mustache of yesteryear. To Meredith Vieira for your wit and remembering who Jon Chattman was. To everyone who shared their wonderful thoughts on the mustache for this book, thanks for your mustache musings. To Venture, thanks for believing in this book when it seemed no one else did. In no particular order, extra special thanks to Mike DiScuillo, Andrew Plotkin, Allie Tarantino, Shira Tarantino, and all of our friends and others who supported our mustache cravings with open arms. Lastly, to Anthony DeCicco, thank you for your inspiration.

Above all else, we'd like to thank those who've embraced the notion that one should never underestimate the power of the mustache. To the stars with 'staches, keep rocking them. To those who've embraced the re-emergence of the "bert," try growing one. To those young kids waiting for their facial hair to grow in. Be patient. It will come.

but wait!
there's
more...

A Brief History of the Mustache

April 14, 1865
John Wilkes Booth alters American history by busting a cap in Abe Lincoln's dome.

May 2, 1876
Ross Barnes hits the National League's first-ever home run.

September 18, 1901
Gillette founded the American Safety Razor Company and manufactured its first razor in 1903.

January 24, 1908
Robert Baden-Powell begins the Boy Scout movement.

June 27, 1940
Captain Kangaroo turns 13.

July 27, 1940
Bugs Bunny, voiced by Mel Blanc makes his official debut in the animated cartoon *A Wild Hare.*

September 14, 1955
Push-broomed "Little Richard" Penniman records his first hit record "Tutti Frutti" and the opening line, "Womp-bomp-a-loom-op-a-womp-bam-boom," is etched in our minds forever.

January 18, 1975
Sherman Hemsley a.k.a. George Jefferson moves on up to the East Side.

March 26, 1976
The Toronto Blue Jays are created, leading the way for fellow 'stache supporters George Bell, Otto Velez, and Roy Howell, just to name a few.

May 21, 1980

Pre-Colt 45 Billy Dee Williams introduces Cloud City to the galaxy in *The Empire Strikes Back*.

June 10, 1983

Gobo's Uncle, Traveling Matt, leaves the Fraggles behind and ventures into "outer space" for the first time.

January 26, 1986

Mike Ditka becomes the first coach in NFL history to win the Super Bowl with a future pro wrestler, a "refrigerator," and of course, a mustache.

June 29, 1988

Eddie Murphy's royal penis is cleaned in the opening scene of *Coming to America*.

September 24, 1988

Canadian sprinter Ben Johnson tests positive for steroids seventeen years before Rafael Palmeiro points his finger at the U.S. Congress.

December 17, 1989

Santa's Little Helper comes in dead last, but more importantly, Simpson's neighbor Ned Flanders makes his animated debut in "Simpsons Roasting on an Open Fire," also known as "The Simpsons Christmas Special."

June 2, 1989

In an attempt to boost Hulk Hogan's acting career Vince McMahon produces the film *No Holds Barred*, which also costars another mustached wrestling monster known as Zeus played by Tommy "Tiny" Lister.

July 4, 1990

Lead by Luther "Uncle Luke" Campbell, 2 Live Crew releases "Banned in the USA"; the lyrics quote "The Star Spangled Banner" and the Gettysburg Address.

February 4, 1993

Leroy Neiman unveils his painting of fellow mustache brother Larry Bird at the Boston Garden.

August 1, 1993

Reggie Jackson is inducted into the MLB Hall of Fame. So much for "killing the queen."

September 28, 1994

Pre–Captain Jack Sparrow Johnny Depp stars with Bill Murray and George "The Animal" Steele in *Ed Wood* with an angora sweater and pencil-thin mustache.

August 6, 1997

As Lt. Moe Tilden, a mustachioed Robert De Niro utters the line "cupcake" in *Copland*.

August 31, 1997

George Steinbrenner's Evil Empire retires Don Mattingly's #23 Jersey despite "Donnie Baseball's" lack of World Series rings. Mattingly, however, joins Monument Park with one hell of a Gold Glove mustache.

February 1, 2003

Morgan Spurlock changes the course of fast food history when he begins his thirty-day McDonald's diet in which he gains 24.5 pounds and an Academy Award nomination for his film *Super Size Me*.

September 20, 2005

Karma is a funny thing, but then again so is Jason Lee's mustache. *My Name Is Earl* makes its television debut.

April 1, 2008

Jon and Rich hit the city for "April Fuzz Day," handing out fake mustaches to over a thousand New Yorkers.

April 11, 2008

Keanu Reeves stars in the *Training Day* knock-off *Street Kings*, which features strong mustached-performances by Forrest Whitaker and even Jay Mohr.

January 15, 2009

Chesley "Sully" Sullenberger safely lands a US Airways plane into the Hudson River giving new meaning to the term "mustache ride."

January 18, 2009

The Wrestler director Darren Aronofsky flashes the 'stache and flips the bird at Mickey Rourke during the actor's acceptance speech for Best Actor at the 66th Annual Golden Globes.

August 21, 2009

Brad Pitt, a man who already has declared he wants to bring back the mustache, sports one in *Inglourious Basterds*. Nazis + Quentin Tarantino + Mustaches = Box Office Gold?

What Stars Say about 'Staches

Author and TheCheapPop.com's Jon Chattman asks the hard questions. In his interviews with celebrities, he doesn't split hairs over their favorite upper-lip follicles. Here's what they have to say:

"The underappreciated 'stache? Cheech Marin."
—Paul Rudd, star of *Anchorman* and *Knocked Up*

"I don't like Bob Dylan's mustache, but that's neither here nor there. I like Martin Mull's mustache. I'm not a big Martin Mull fan, but he's got a good mustache. I like a blond mustache."
—Michael Cera, *Arrested Development*, *Superbad*, and *Juno*

"As a proud Italian man, I've tried to grow a mustache several times over the past twenty years, but I've never been able to equal my grandmother's. The best mustache in history is Thurman Munson's. He just looked really cool in the '70s with a mustache as a catcher for the Yankees. He's my favorite player, so I think people should buy this book because some of the coolest people in history have had mustaches. Munson . . . Rollie Fingers . . . a 1977 version of Burt Reynolds . . . Golda Meir."
—Artie Lange, *The Howard Stern Show*

"I'm the only one who can cut my mustache the right way. I'm from the world of the little French mustache. I use a little Bic razor, and believe it or not, I'm so precise and excellent cutting my own. A little disposable razor goes a long way; you just got to know what you're doing. I could open a little barbershop and just do mustaches. You can't find one loose strand anywhere. It's tight, man. No one cuts a mustache like me."

—J. B. Smoove, *Curb Your Enthusiasm*

"Frank Zappa had a great mustache, because it was a full-on and unapologetic mustache. It was mustache with a capital M. [On why there aren't any mustaches on the island] We've got some shaggy-looking guys. Sawyer's a little shaggy. Jack gets the full mustache and beard thing going in the future. Sayid. Oh you mean just mustache? I think the feeling is aesthetically it appears to be groomed. You have a mustache with no beard it implies that you spent time cultivating the mustache and not cultivating the beard, which is a little too sort of self-conscious for the designers."

—Michael Emerson, *Lost*

"There is not a day in the 365 calendar year that I don't need to look like an angry Freddie Mercury. Criminals beware I just might 'Bohemian Rhapsody' your ass."

—Carlos Alazraqui, Deputy James Garcia on *Reno 911!*

"'You're pretty much the only kid in school who can grow a mustache.' Napoleon says that to Pedro. Funny stuff. Every character, every man has their days of being barbarous."

—Efren Ramirez, *Napoleon Dynamite*

"I like all kinds of mustaches. There's the old cavalier mustache . . . that's always a good look. I would say the 1930s look for mustaches were pretty good. The movie, *The Thin Man*, and the Powell look. But you have to have the right kind of shaped head for certain mustaches. You can try and go for something you like.

Over the centuries, I've had to adjust. I've never actually cultivated a mustache. I just simply have a mustache."

—Leon Redbone, mustachioed singer

"I have a deep respect for anyone who can make a mustache work. It takes a man to grow a beard, but it takes a bold man to shave that beard off and leave the mustache on his face. . . . I've always been partial to the solid upper-lip work of Tom Selleck, and I know I was not the only one who grieved when he went smooth for *In and Out*. But for sheer audacity, bushy manliness, and latte foam retention potential, I have to go with Sam Elliott. It's difficult to think about mustaches without thinking of Sam Elliott, but it is almost impossible to think of Sam Elliott without thinking of mustaches."

—Jonathan Coulton

"The cover of *Sgt. Pepper* says it all. Paul's mustache is perfect, also Dennis Hopper's in *Easy Rider*."

—Ileana Douglas, *Cape Fear*, *To Die For*, and *Ghost World*

"Ben Turpin's was the mother of all mustaches."

—Joseph R. Gannascoli, *The Sopranos*

"The mustache is a beautiful thing because it's perfect proof that looking like every of-age girl's father from when they were four really works."

—Jesse Hughes, Eagles of Death Metal

"Tom Selleck easily or Rollie Fingers. I think Tom Selleck is probably the only man alive that actually looks good with a mustache, and Rollie Fingers it was part of his character to have a mustache. Anybody named Rollie Fingers has to have a handlebar mustache."

—John Rocker, former Major League Baseball relief pitcher

Below my nose there was a void
Above the upper lip
I tried to grow a 'stache of must
And waxed it at the tip
I thought it made me look so cool
So worldly and worn
I looked just like a movie star
Who was confined to porn

—"A Mustache Poem" by
Lanny "The Genius" Poffo, pro wrestler

Bonus Berts—Extended 'Stache Lists

Top 100 Celluloid 'Staches

1. Sam Elliott, *The Big Lebowski*
2. Jeff Daniels, *Gettysburg*
3. Sean Connery, *Zardoz*
4. Daniel Day-Lewis, *Gangs of New York*
5. Burt Reynolds, *Cannonball Run II*
6. Cheech Marin, *Up in Smoke*
7. Tom Selleck, *Mr. Baseball*
8. Matt Dillon, *There's Something about Mary*
9. Harry Shearer, *This Is Spinal Tap*
10. Clark Gable, *Gone with the Wind*
11. Charles Bronson, *The Mechanic*
12. Benecio Del Toro, *Fear and Loathing in Las Vegas*
13. George Clooney, *O Brother, Where Art Thou?*
14. Elliott Gould, *Busting*
15. Terry-Thomas, *Those Magnificent Men in Their Flying Machines*
16. Oliver Reed, *Women in Love*
17. Carl Weathers, *Action Jackson*
18. Nicolas Cage, *Raising Arizona*
19. Charlie Chaplin, *City Lights*
20. John Wayne, *The Conqueror*
21. Marlon Brando, *The Godfather*
22. Vincent Price, *The Tingler*
23. Richard Roundtree, *Shaft*
24. Dermot Mulroney, *About Schmidt*
25. Wilford Brimley, *Cocoon*
26. Jason Patric, *Narc*

27. Ben Stiller, *Dodgeball*
28. Kevin Spacey, *Midnight in the Garden of Good and Evil*
29. William H. Macy, *Boogie Nights*
30. Gene Wilder, *Young Frankenstein*
31. Sacha Baron Cohen, *Borat*
32. Kevin Costner, *Dances with Wolves*
33. Robert De Niro, *Copland*
34. Will Ferrell, *Anchorman: The Legend of Ron Burgandy*
35. Richard Pryor, *Superman III*
36. Bob Hoskins, *Super Mario Bros.*
37. Richard Harris, *Major Dundee*
38. Gene Kelly, *The Pirate*
39. Kevin Kline, *A Fish Called Wanda*
40. Matthew McConaughey, *Dazed and Confused*
41. Rudy Ray Moore, *Dolemite*
42. David Koechner, *Out Cold*
43. Bruce Dern, *Coming Home*
44. Efren Ramirez, *Napoleon Dynamite*
45. Danny Trejo, *Once upon a Time in Mexico*
46. Michael Jeter, *Air Bud*
47. Groucho Marx, *Duck Soup*
48. Morgan Freeman, *Driving Miss Daisy*
49. Peter Boyle, *Where the Buffalo Roam*
50. Tom Cruise, *Born on the Fourth of July*
51. Jack Nicholson, *The Last Detail*
52. Emilio Estevez, *Stakeout*
53. Danny Glover, *Lethal Weapon*
54. Nick Nolte, *North Dallas Forty*
55. Val Kilmer, *Tombstone*
56. Peter Ustinov, *Evil under the Sun*

57. Pat Morita, *Collision Course*
58. Jeff Bridges, *American Heart*
59. Philippe Noiret, *Cinema Paradiso*
60. Billy Dee Williams, *The Empire Strikes Back*
61. Lee J. Cobb, *The Exorcist*
62. Timothy Dalton, *Flash Gordon*
63. Dabney Coleman, *9 to 5*
64. Harvey Keitel, *U-571*
65. Peter Sellers, *Dr. Strangelove*
66. Edward James Olmos, *The Ballad of Gregorio Cortez*
67. Donald Sutherland, *Space Cowboys*
68. Kiefer Sutherland, *The Cowboy Way*
69. Pedro Gonzalez Gonzalez, *Rio Bravo*
70. Jake Gyllenhaal, *Brokeback Mountain*
71. Marcello Mastroianni, *Divorzio all'italiana*
72. Charles "Mayor of Munchkin City" Becker, *The Wizard of Oz*
73. Johnny Depp, *Donnie Brasco*
74. Jack Albertson, *Willy Wonka and the Chocolate Factory*
75. Alan Hale, *Desperate Journey*
76. Paul Newman, *The Color of Money*
77. David Arquette, *Scream*
78. Pat Hingle, *Splendor in the Grass*
79. Prince, *Purple Rain*
80. Martin Scorsese, *The Age of Innocence*
81. Richard Dreyfuss, *Night Falls on Manhattan*
82. Dustin Hoffman, *Hook*
83. Robert Duvall, *Geronimo*
84. Gregory Peck, *Old Gringo*
85. Jon Lovitz, *A League of Their Own*
86. Chris Cooper, *Adaptation*

87. Dennis Farina, *Out of Sight*
88. David Bowie, *The Prestige*
89. Mel Brooks, *Spaceballs*
90. Steve Zahn, *Bandidas*
91. Noah Taylor, *The Life Aquatic with Steve Zissou*
92. John Candy, *Planes, Trains, and Automobiles*
93. Lou Gossett Jr., *An Officer and a Gentleman*
94. Seth Rogen, *Superbad*
95. John Travolta, *The Thin Red Line*
96. Billy Crudup, *Almost Famous*
97. Patrick Swayze, *Tall Tale*
98. Thomas Jane, *Original Sin*
99. William Forsythe, *Out for Justice*
100. Gene Hackman, *The Royal Tenenbaums*

Top 100 Sports 'Staches

1. Rollie Fingers, Baseball
2. Lanny McDonald, Hockey
3. Mark Spitz, Swimming
4. Dick Butkus, Football
5. Richard Petty, Racing
6. John L. Sullivan, Boxing
7. Humberto Coelho, Soccer
8. Keith Hernandez, Baseball
9. Greg Kite, Basketball
10. Ross Grimsley, Baseball
11. Mike Schmidt, Baseball
12. Dale Earnhardt, Racing
13. Larry Csonka, Football

14. Kurt Rambis, Basketball
15. Dale Berra, Baseball
16. John Ball Jr., Golf
17. Don Aase, Baseball
18. Buck Ewing, Baseball
19. Alexis Arguello, Boxing
20. Willie Hernandez, Baseball
21. Rod Beck, Baseball
22. William Perry, Football
23. Jim "Catfish" Hunter, Baseball
24. Denis Savard, Hockey
25. Dennis Eckersley, Baseball
26. John Naber, Swimming
27. Dan Dierdorf, Football
28. Carmen Fanzone, Baseball
29. Julius Erving, Basketball
30. Phil Jackson, Basketball
31. Luis Tiant, Baseball
32. Warren Moon, Football
33. Eddie Murray, Baseball
34. Walter Payton, Football
35. Joe Dumars, Basketball
36. Frank Viola, Baseball
37. Larry Little, Football
38. Pete Vukovich, Baseball
39. Albert Spalding, Baseball
40. Rocky Belier, Football
41. Charles Barkley, Basketball
42. Cap Anson, Baseball
43. Jesse Barfield, Baseball

44. Wade Boggs, Baseball
45. John Clarkson, Baseball
46. Jim Rice, Baseball
47. Rod Langway, Hockey
48. King Kelly, Baseball
49. Rick Mahorn, Basketball
50. Gerry Coetzee, Boxing
51. Patrick Ewing, Basketball
52. Roberto Duran, Boxing
53. Reggie Jackson, Baseball
54. George Foreman, Boxing
55. Adam Morrison, Basketball
56. Don Baylor, Baseball
57. Jack Morris, Baseball
58. Bobby Bonilla, Baseball
59. Bill Nyrop, Hockey
60. Michael Spinks, Boxing
61. Jerry Remy, Baseball
62. Randy White, Football
63. George Parros, Hockey
64. Jerry Morales, Baseball
65. Tim Foli, Baseball
66. Bob Dailey, Hockey
67. Ray Mansfield, Football
68. Dale Sveum, Baseball
69. Phil McConkey, Football
70. Wilfredo Benitez, Boxing
71. Jorge Bell, Baseball
72. Dan Quisenberry, Baseball
73. Art Monk, Football

74. Dave Steib, Baseball
75. Al Bumbry, Baseball
76. AC Green, Basketball
77. Oscar Gamble, Baseball
78. Ken Norton, Boxing
79. Gorman Thomas, Baseball
80. Jim Brown, Football
81. Sparky Lyle, Baseball
82. Ralph Sampson, Basketball
83. Barry Foote, Baseball
84. Ron Cey, Baseball
85. Ruppert Jones, Baseball
86. Alex English, Basketball
87. Randy Johnson, Baseball
88. Davy Lopes, Baseball
89. Jeffrey Leonard, Baseball
90. Mark Gastineau, Football
91. Robin Yount, Baseball
92. Jim O'Rourke, Baseball
93. Rico Carty, Baseball
94. Ron Guidry, Baseball
95. Eugene Upshaw, Football
96. Tim Witherspoon, Boxing
97. Reggie Roby, Football
98. Dan Gladden, Baseball
99. Vida Blue, Baseball
100. King Gustav V, Golf

Top 40 Musical 'Staches

1. John Oates, Hall and Oates
2. David Crosby
3. Freddie Mercury
4. Jim Croce
5. Sonny Bono
6. Frank Zappa
7. Glenn Hughes, The Village People
8. Lionel Richie
9. John Bonham, Led Zeppelin
10. Duane Allman, The Allman Brothers
11. Tony Orlando
12. El DeBarge
13. Dave Mason, Traffic
14. Sammy Davis, Jr.
15. Lee Hazlewood
16. Prince
17. Chuck Berry
18. Larry Blackmon, Cameo
19. Ben E. King
20. Ike Turner
21. Bob Dylan
22. Baris Manco
23. Ringo Starr
24. Luther Vandross
25. James Taylor
26. Wayne Newton
27. Carlos Santana
28. Errol Brown, Hot Chocolate

29. "Weird Al" Yankovic
30. Ray Parker Jr.
31. Victor Borge
32. Alan Jackson
33. Fats Domino
34. Little Richard
35. Robert Goulet
36. James Hetfield
37. Cab Calloway
38. Stevie Wonder
39. Will Smith
40. Jimmy Buffett

Top 50 'Staches We Tuned In To

1. Tom Selleck, *Magnum P.I.*
2. Burt Reynolds, *Evening Shade*
3. Geraldo Rivera
4. Rob Reiner, *All in the Family*
5. Christopher Hewitt, *Mr. Belvedere*
6. Dennis Weaver, *McCloud*
7. Desmond Wilson, *Sanford and Son*
8. Roscoe Orman, *Sesame Street*
9. John Ratzenberger, *Cheers*
10. Captain Kangaroo
11. Sherman Hemsley, *The Jeffersons*
12. Gabe Kaplan, *Welcome Back, Kotter*
13. Jason Lee, *My Name Is Earl*
14. David White, *Bewitched*
15. John Astin, *The Addams Family*

16. Buddy Ebsen, *The Beverly Hillbillies*
17. Alex Trebek, *Jeopardy!*
18. Arsenio Hall, *The Arsenio Hall Show*
19. Doc Severinsen, *The Tonight Show*
20. John Stossell, *20/20*
21. Dr. Phil McGraw
22. Walter Cronkite
23. Ted Lange, *The Love Boat*
24. Stacy Keach, *Mike Hammer*
25. Jeffrey Tambor, *The Larry Sanders Show*
26. Judge Joe Brown
27. Dick Van Dyke, *Diagnosis Murder*
28. Dick Wilson, Charmin commercials
29. Ian McShane, *Deadwood*
30. Pat Harrington, *One Day at a Time*
31. Alex Karras, *Webster*
32. Eric Braeden, *One Life to Live*
33. Freddie Prinze, *Chico and the Man*
34. Fred the Baker, Dunkin' Donuts commercials
35. Dick Butkus, *My Two Dads*
36. Dennis Franz, *NYPD Blue*
37. Keenan Ivory Wayans, *In Living Color*
38. Carl Lumbly, *Cagney and Lacey*
39. Dick Martin, *Laugh-In*
40. Len Lesser, "Uncle Leo," *Seinfeld*
41. Howard Hesseman, *Head of the Class*
42. Wilfred Brimley, *Our House*
43. Jimmie Walker, *Good Times*
44. Hal Williams, *227*
45. John Cleese, *Fawlty Towers*

46. Jerry Colonna, *The Jerry Colonna Show*
47. Graham Nelson, BBC, *Secret Army*
48. Don Ramon, *Chavo Del Ocho*
49. Howard Keel, *Dallas*
50. Theodore "Teddy" Wilson, *That's My Mama*

'Stache Trivia

1. Which actor starred in the long-running television series *Beverly Hillbillies,* in which he played family patriarch Jed Clampett?

    A. Bob Denver

    B. Buddy Ebsen

    C. Buddy Lembeck

    D. Carl "Oldy" Olsen

2. William Marshall appeared in what blaxploitation flick about an African Prince who visits Transylvania?

    A. *Dolemite*

    B. *Abbott and Costello Meet Frankenstein*

    C. *Blacula*

    D. *Interview with a Vampire*

3. What was the name of Jesse "The Body" Ventura's character in *The Running Man,* which also starred Arnold Schwarzenegger and *Family Feud*'s Richard Dawson?

    A. Captain Planet

    B. Subzero

    C. Glacier

    D. Captain Freedom

4. Fast-talking John Moschitta Jr. appeared in commercials for which toy during the mid-1980s?

    A. Voltron

    B. Stretch Armstrong

    C. Micro Machines

    D. My Little Pony

5. Who was best known for his Emmy-nominated role as Captain Barney Miller?

    A. Abe Vigoda

    B. Lou Ferrigno

    C. Hal Linden

    D. Harry Bentley

6. Pat Harrington played Schneider the apartment super for which prime-time comedy-drama show?

    A. *Tales of the Gold Monkey*

    B. *Days of Our Lives*

    C. *CHiPs*

    D. *One Day at a Time*

7. Which two actors played Gotham City's mustached Commissioner Gordon?

    A. Ed Begley Jr. and Ed Asner

    B. Gary Coleman and Pat Sajak

    C. Gary Oldman and Pat Hingle

    D. Treat Williams and Danny Glover

8. In which of the following films did Sean Connery *not* have a mustache?

    A. *Zardoz*

    B. *The Untouchables*

    C. *First Knight*

    D. *A Good Man in Africa*

9. Which wrestler never had a mustache in the ring?
    A. Ric Flair
    B. Magnum T.A.
    C. Scott Hall
    D. Junkyard Dog

10. Which one of these cinematic mustaches were fake?
    A. Kevin Spacey, *Midnight in the Garden of Good and Evil*
    B. Sam Elliott, *The Golden Compass*
    C. Billy Burke, *Twilight*
    D. Glenn Close, *Hook*

11. Which group has *not* had a mustached man on their album cover?
    A. Hall & Oates
    B. The New Pornographers
    C. Weezer
    D. Led Zeppelin

12. What was the name of the mustached character Ben Stiller played in *Dodgeball?*
    A. Black Thunder
    B. White Goodman
    C. Dwight Gooden
    D. John Goodman

13. Which of these mustaches don't belong?
    A. Wilford Brimley
    B. Sam Elliott
    C. William H. Taft
    D. John Waters

14. Which of these New York Mets mustaches was not actually real?
    A. Keith Hernandez
    B. Jose Valentin
    C. Bobby Valentine
    D. Davey Johnson

15. True or False: Captain Lou Albano had a mustache in more than one movie.

16. True or False: Omar Sharif won the Best Actor Oscar for his starring role in *Doctor Zhivago*.

17. True or False: Frank Beard is the only member of ZZ Top with a mustache and not a beard.

18. True or False: Jim Carrey's mustache was real in *The Cable Guy*.

19. True or False: Franklin D. Roosevelt was the last president to have a mustache.

20. Please write in 100 words or less, who has had the greatest mustache of all time.

_____

_____

_____

_____

_____

Answers

1-B, 2-C, 3-D, 4-C, 5-C, 6-D, 7-C, 8-C, 9-A, 10-D, 11-D, 12-B, 13-D, 14-C, 15-True, 16-False, 17-True, 18-False, 19-False; 20-You're right!

About the Authors

JON CHATTMAN has interviewed some of the most respected personalities in the entertainment business, from Alf to Paul Newman. For over eleven years, he has written on all walks of pop culture specializing in film, television, and music, and has previously worked as a managing newspaper editor and a local beat reporter. For over three years, Chattman has owned and operated TheCheapPop.com, a pop culture humor site that specializes in down-to-earth celebrity interviews, entertainment reviews, and mustache-centric content. His writings have appeared in the *New York Post*, *Wizard*, AOL's Spinner.com, the *Huffington Post*, and *TV Guide* to name a few. Throughout his career, he has received numerous acknowledgments including several writing awards from the New York Press Association (NYPA). Chattman is also the coauthor of *Rock-On! An Anthology of Concert Memories* with Ellen Rosner Feig. When not writing, he enjoys working out, listening to music, going to the movies, watching television, and re-enacting classic *Golden Girls* episodes with his stuffed animals. He currently resides in Westchester County, New York, with his wife and no dogs.

RICH TARANTINO has worked in the education field for over ten years. He has moonlighted as a freelance photographer and has contributed articles and graphic design work for TheCheapPop.com, which he helped get off the ground. When he's not wearing a wrestling mask, he can be found playing Wiffle ball in his parents' backyard. He currently resides in Westchester County, New York, with his wife and one dog.

About the Illustrator

BRETT UNDERHILL is an illustrator and animator whose bed, couch, and floor lamp are currently located in beautiful Brooklyn, New York. His shorts and illustration portfolio can be viewed at *www.porkchopbob.com*, as well as within the pages of the occasional lost moleskin notepad.